MW01413285

PRESENTING
Kathryn Lasky

Twayne's United States Authors Series
Young Adult Authors

Patricia J. Campbell, General Editor

TUSAS 708

KATHRYN LASKY IN HER STUDY, CAMBRIDGE, MASSACHUSETTS
Chris Knight

PRESENTING

Kathryn Lasky

Joanne Brown

Twayne Publishers
An Imprint of Simon & Schuster Macmillan
New York

Prentice Hall International
London Mexico City New Delhi Singapore Sydney Toronto

Twayne's United States Authors Series No. 708

Presenting Kathryn Lasky
Joanne Brown

Copyright © 1998 by Twayne Publishers
All rights reserved. No part of this book may be reproduced or transmitted in any form or by any means, electronic or mechanical, including photocopying, recording, or by any information storage and retrieval system, without permission in writing from the Publisher.

Twayne Publishers
An Imprint of Simon & Schuster Macmillan
1633 Broadway
New York, NY 10019

Library of Congress Cataloging-in-Publication Data

Brown, Joanne, 1933–
    Presenting Kathryn Lasky / Joanne Brown.
      p. cm. — (Twayne's United States authors series ; TUSAS 708. Young adult authors)
    Includes bibliographical references (p.) and index.
    ISBN 0-8057-1677-7 (alk. paper)
    1. Lasky, Kathryn—Criticism and interpretation. 2. Young adult fiction, American—History and criticism. 3. Women and literature—United States—History—20th century. I. Title. II. Series: Twayne's United States authors series ; TUSAS 708. III. Series: Twayne's United States authors series. Young adult authors.
PS3562.A75259Z57   1998
813'.54—dc21   98-35177
                                                                                 CIP

This paper meets the requirements of ANSI/NISO Z3948-1992 (Permanence of Paper).

10 9 8 7 6 5 4 3 2 1

Printed in the United States of America

To Milt
loving husband, best friend

Contents

LIST OF ILLUSTRATIONS	ix
FOREWORD	xi
PREFACE	xiii
CHRONOLOGY	xvii

1.	Searching for Kathryn Lasky: The Early Years	1
2.	Searching for Kathryn Lasky: The Writer	23
3.	Toads in the Garden: Kathryn Lasky's Approach to Historical Fiction	47
4.	Smelling the Rat: Journeys into the Nineteenth Century	68
5.	Contemporary Lives: Family and Friends	102
6.	Danger: Zealots at Work	131
7.	Searching for Kathryn Lasky: Epilogue	151

NOTES AND REFERENCES	153
SELECTED BIBLIOGRAPHY	160
INDEX	167

Illustrations

1. Kathryn Lasky in her study, Cambridge, Massachusetts ... ii
2. Kathy's first photo opportunity, with parents and sister Martha, then five ... 2
3. Kathy in Florida, age five ... 8
4. Kathy, age seven ... 9
5. Chris and Kathy in Maine, on the occasion of their engagement ... 11
6. Kathy at work in her study ... 22
7. Aunt Ann Lasky Smith, the real Nana Sashie ... 59
8. Kathy hiking out west, collecting images for her western historical fiction ... 69
9. Kathy at a book signing ... 150
10. The Knight family: Max, Kathy, Chris, and Meribah, November 1997 ... 150

Foreword

The advent of Twayne's Young Adult Authors series in 1985 was a response to the growing stature and value of adolescent literature and the lack of serious critical evaluation of the new genre. The first volume of the series was heralded as marking the coming-of-age of young adult fiction.

The aim of the series is twofold. First, it enables young readers to research the work of their favorite authors and to see them as real people. Each volume is written in a lively, readable style and attempts to present in an attractive, accessible format a vivid portrait of the author as a person.

Second, the series provides teachers and librarians with insights and background material for promoting and teaching young adult novels. Each of the biocritical studies is a serious literary analysis of one author's work (or one subgenre within young adult literature), with attention to plot structure, theme, character, setting, and imagery. In addition, many of the series writers delve deeper into the creative writing process by tracking down early drafts or unpublished manuscripts by their subjects, consulting with their subjects' editors or other mentors, and examining influences from literature, film, or social movements.

Many of the authors contributing to the series are among the leading scholars and critics of adolescent literature. Some are even novelists themselves for young adults. Most of the studies are based on extensive interviews with the subject author, and each includes an exhaustive study of his or her work. Although the general format of the series is the same, the individual volumes are uniquely shaped by their subjects, and each brings a different perspective to the classroom.

The goal of the series is to produce a succinct but comprehensive study of the life and art of every leading writer for young adults, to trace how that art has been accepted by readers and critics, and to evaluate its place in the developing field of adolescent literature. And—perhaps most important—the series is intended to inspire a reading and rereading of this quality fiction that speaks so directly to young people about their life experiences.

Patricia J. Campbell,
General Editor

Preface

San Diego, 1995: a session at the Assembly on Literature for Adolescents, an annual postconference workshop following the conference of the National Council of Teachers of English. The woman on the podium spoke with an engaging mixture of intensity and levity. Her subject was censorship, and as she addressed the large crowd of conference participants I found myself nodding in agreement, smiling at her wry humor. She was taking deadly aim at zealots of all varieties, those on the left as well as those on the right, her scorn matched only by her wit. She was someone I wished I knew. She was Kathryn Lasky.

At the break following the session, I stood in the line for coffee talking with Patty Campbell, general editor of the Twayne's Young Adult Authors series. We often exchanged pleasantries at the workshop, sometimes about a recent Twayne publication, sometimes about an article on YA literature I had published. Today, we traded responses to the session we had just attended, both of us enthusiastic about the speech and the speaker. "If you ever decide to do a Twayne book on Kathryn Lasky—" I began. Before I could finish, Patty Campbell said, "Would you be interested in writing a book on Kathryn Lasky?"

My quick affirmative introduced me to a project whose proportions I hardly suspected at the time. I had read two or three of Lasky's young adult novels and knew that she had written others. However, I had not anticipated the sheer volume of her work: dozens of children's books and nearly two dozen novels, including nine novels for young adults. In the months that I worked on this project, her list of publications grew steadily: she published several critical articles and 10 more books, including one of her best historical novels for young adults. Along the way, she garnered two national book awards.

Kathryn Lasky proved not only prolific but versatile. She writes in many genres and for readers of many ages—picture books for children, lengthy novels for adults, fiction and science and biography and mystery. She blurs the lines between genres: imaginary scenes enliven her nonfiction, and her fiction brims with detailed information. As a writer for young adults, she is perhaps best known for her American historical fiction, but she is now working on a novel about Robin Hood told from Maid Marian's point of view. Her writer's ingenuity has discovered subjects that range from butterflies and dinosaurs to literary ghosts and puppets; her ideas traverse boundaries of culture, geography, and time. As I made my way through her work, trying to construct a coherent whole, she continued to produce book after book, sometimes in a new genre, always on a new subject. My notes developed into a series of question marks, and my conclusions seemed more problematic with each new publication.

Of late, critics and educators have engaged in heated discussion about exploding the literary canon and loosening the hold of "dead white males" on it. There is this, though, to say for that maligned group: they are safely departed, their work complete and neatly shelved. However readers may construct or deconstruct their work, these writers will produce nothing new that calls into question any critical commentary about it. Kathryn Lasky, very much alive and prolific, offers no such assurance. On the other hand, she extends invitations for dinner at her home, sits willingly for extended periods answering questions into a tape recorder, and shares with candid good humor private glimpses into her personal life.

In fact, no one could ask for a better subject than Kathryn Lasky Knight. On my copy of *True North* she wrote, "To Joanne, who must surely be bored to tears with me." Not a chance. Many adjectives might describe a response to this spirited writer, but "bored" is not among them. Anne Reit, Lasky's editor at Scholastic Press, says of her, "There are some writers you make a real connection with. Kathy is one of those." I, too, feel "connected" to Kathryn Lasky. I am deeply grateful to her for the unflagging cooperation and enthusiasm that she brought to each interview, and to her husband, Chris Knight, who provided not only helpful insights but professional photographs. My thanks, too, to Patty Campbell for encouraging me to undertake this project and for her editorial guidance along the way. I would also like to express my appreciation to Drake University's Center for the Humanities for granting me release time to complete this project. Without its support, I never could have finished on schedule.

Chronology

1944 Kathryn Lasky born 24 June to Hortense and Marven Lasky in Indianapolis.

1952 Enrolls in Tudor Hall, private school for girls.

1962 Graduates from Tudor Hall and enrolls in the University of Michigan.

1966 Graduates from the University of Michigan with a B.A. in English. Returns to Indianapolis to work as substitute teacher. Tours Europe after end of school year.

1967 Goes to New York, takes job at *Town and Country* magazine. Resigns job and moves to Cambridge, Massachusetts. Enrolls as part-time student in Harvard University's Divinity School.

1968 Meets Christopher Knight.

1971 Marries Christopher Knight. Begins married life in Cambridge.

1972 Moves to brownstone home overlooking Boston's harbor. Makes "bargain in the sky" with Knight by agreeing to sail to Europe and back on their 30-foot ketch *Leucothea* if Knight will give up flying.

1974 Sails to Europe on *Leucothea* and spends summer there. Leaves ketch in Europe and returns to States in fall. Enrolls in Wheelock College to earn master's degree as a reading specialist. Begins to contribute articles to *Sail* magazine.

xvii

1975	Returns with Knight to Europe for summer and sails *Leucothea* on European waterways. Continues at Wheelock during school year, also working as freelance writer. Publishes articles in *Sail* magazine.
1976	Sails *Leucothea* home. Publishes *I Have Four Names for My Grandfather*, her first collaboration with Chris Knight, whose photographs illustrate the book. Graduates from Wheelock College with a master's in reading.
1977	Son, Max, born in December. Publishes *Tugboats Never Sleep*, children's picture book.
1978	Publishes *Tall Ships*, her first book of children's nonfiction.
1979	Moves to Newton, Massachusetts. Publishes *My Island Grandmother*, children's picture book.
1980	Moves back to Cambridge.
1981	Publishes first two of four children's books on traditional crafts: *The Weaver's Gift*, an ALA Notable Book for Children, and *Dollmaker: The Eyelight and the Shadow*. Wins Boston Globe–Horn Book Award for Nonfiction for body of her work.
1982	Daughter, Meribah, born in August. Publishes first YA novel, *The Night Journey*, an ALA Notable Book for Young Adults and winner of the National Jewish Book Award for Children; and *Jem's Island*, children's fiction.
1983	Publishes *Beyond the Divide*, an ALA Best Book for Young Adults and a *New York Times* Notable Book; and *Sugaring Time*, children's nonfiction, named as a Newbery Honor Book and an ALA Notable Book for Children.
1984	Publishes *Prank*, an ALA Best Book for Young Adults; and *A Baby for Max*, children's picture book.
1985	Purchases home on Deer Isle, Maine. Publishes *Atlantic Circle*, nonfiction for adults; *Home Free*, YA novel; and

Chronology

      Puppeteer, children's nonfiction, designated as an ALA Notable Book for Children.

1986 Publishes *Pageant,* an ALA Notable Book for Young Adults; and *Trace Elements,* a Calista Jacobs mystery for adults.

1988 Publishes *The Bone Wars,* YA novel; and *Sea Swan,* illustrated children's fiction.

1989 Publishes *Traces of Life: The Origins of Humankind,* nonfiction children's book; and *Widow of Oz,* adult novel. Death of mother, Hortense Lasky.

1990 Publishes *Dinosaur Dig,* children's nonfiction; and *Mortal Words,* a Calista Jacobs mystery for adults.

1991 Publishes *Fourth of July Bear,* children's picture book; *Double Trouble Squared,* first Starbuck adventure novel; *Mumbo Jumbo,* Calista Jacobs mystery for adults.

1992 Publishes *Shadows in the Water,* Starbuck adventure novel; *I Have an Aunt on Marlborough Street,* children's picture book; and *Surtsey: The Newest Place on Earth,* children's nonfiction.

1993 Publishes *A Voice in the Wind,* Starbuck adventure novel; *The Tantrum,* children's picture book; and *Searching for Laura Ingalls: A Reader's Journey* and *Monarchs,* children's nonfiction.

1994 Publishes *Memoirs of a Bookbat* and *Beyond the Burning Time,* YA novels; *Cloud Eyes,* children's picture book; *Days of the Dead* and *The Librarian Who Measured the Earth,* children's nonfiction; and *Dark Swan,* Calista Jacobs mystery for adults.

1995 Publishes *Pond Year* and *Gates of the Wind,* children's picture books; and *She's Wearing a Dead Bird on Her Head,* children's nonfiction.

1996 Publishes *True North,* YA novel; *Lunch Bunnies,* children's picture book; Dear America's *A Journey to the*

New World: The Diary of Remember Patience Whipple, historical fiction for middle-school readers. The novel wins commendation as a Notable Children's Trade Book in the Field of Social Studies, and Dear America wins the Jefferson Cup Award for the best American historical fiction series of 1996.

1997   Publishes *Marven of the Great North Woods,* children's picture book, which won the National Jewish Book Award for Children; *Hercules: The Man, the Myth, the Hero,* children's illustrated fiction; and *The Most Beautiful Roof in the World: Exploring the Rainforest Canopy,* children's nonfiction.

1998   Publishes *Alice Rose and Sam* and Dear America's *Dreams in the Golden Country: The Diary of Zipporah Feldman, a Jewish Immigrant Girl,* both historical novels for middle-school readers; and *Shadows in the Dawn: The Lemurs of Madagascar* and *A Brilliant Streak: The Making of Mark Twain,* children's nonfiction.

1. Searching for Kathryn Lasky: The Early Years

As the author of many books for children and young adults, she is known as "Kathryn Lasky," but her friends and family call her Kathy. The nickname seems more fitting for Lasky's buoyant, irreverent presence. She is slender, with large brown eyes that flash with wit and purpose. Her thick brown hair, streaked with gray, is piled on top of her head, anchored with what she calls "an industrial-strength barrette" and sometimes speared with a pencil. When she speaks, her ideas spill out in a swift current of humor, colloquialisms, and candid admissions. She says her family tree, transplanted from the Jewish shtetls of eastern Europe, is more of a "shrub," usually refers to children as "kids," and admits that she is "addicted" to *People* magazine. "I could probably—if pressed—describe every wedding gown that Elizabeth Taylor ever wore," she says. "There's a trashy part of my mind that just loves that stuff."[1] Although her work is distinguished by scholarly research and a striking range of knowledge, there is nothing stuffy about Kathy Lasky Knight.

In 1993 she published a children's book called *Searching for Laura Ingalls: A Reader's Journey*. It recounts a family vacation during which Lasky, her husband, and their two children visited the sites of Ingalls' homes, the settings for her Little House series. Lasky's daughter, Meribah, had read and loved those books, and the trip throughout the upper Midwest—to South Dakota, Minnesota, and Wisconsin—was spurred by her interest. The narration alternates between Lasky's prose and excerpts from Meribah's journal; photographs by Lasky's husband, Christopher

1

Kathy's first photo opportunity, with parents and sister Martha, then five
Courtesy Kathryn Lasky

Knight, illustrate the journey. Both text and images confirm that this journey deepened Meribah's appreciation of Ingalls' novels. Like Ingalls, Lasky is a popular and prolific writer. Perhaps someday a reader, captivated by her considerable output—more than 50 books to date—will go in search of Kathryn Lasky. Both Lasky's fiction and nonfiction bear the indelible stamp of the places she has lived and visited. Fans of Kathryn Lasky, taking their cue from Meribah, might discover in the scenes of her life a resonance that enhances their responses to her work. Anyone wishing to undertake such a journey should begin in Indianapolis, where Lasky was born on June 24, 1944, and where she lived until she left for college. Her home sat on a large, sloping lot. There was a pond behind the house where Lasky and her best friend spent many hours. Lasky's picture book *Pond Year*, a tribute to friendship as well as an exploration of nature's seasonal changes, recaptures that time and place.

Her mother furnished the house with what Lasky describes as "exquisite taste." Over the years, her parents collected Early American furniture of museum quality, and some of the pieces—a dining set, a desk, a four-poster bed—now grace Lasky's own home in Cambridge, Massachusetts.

Family Background

In many ways, Lasky led an idyllic childhood; she was an adored child (along with her older sister, Martha) of attentive, spirited parents. On the surface, her parents were oddly matched. Her father, Marven, was the son of Russian immigrants who had settled in Duluth, Minnesota.[2] As a child, he developed a sense of adventure and a deep love of the northern woods around Duluth, exploring them during the long winters on a pair of skis that his father had fashioned from barrel staves. Lasky's children's book *Marven of the Great North Woods*, which won the National Jewish Book Award in 1997, tells the true story of her father's experiences during the terrible influenza epidemic of 1918, when his parents sent him to live in a logging camp far from the threat of illness and death. Only 10 years old at the time, Marven was assigned the job of waking the loggers. He also helped to keep the books. Armed with ingenuity and a willingness to work hard, he survived both the experience and the epidemic, making friends with the rough French Canadian loggers and learning their language.

With little formal education past high school, Lasky's father pursued a checkered career as a lifeguard, a caretaker of alligators in a Florida Seminole village, and a salesman, first of ladies' hats and then, after Prohibition, for a liquor company. Eventually he founded his own bottling and distributing company.

Lasky's mother, Hortense, was the child of prosperous parents. They provided a lively, urbane home in Indianapolis for their children, complete with a servant "who functioned as a combination butler-nursemaid-handyman-chauffeur" (*AC*, 30). In their powder blue Model-T Ford they traveled each summer to vacation spots in northern Indiana and on the East Coast. All the children were college educated. Hortense earned a degree in social work and obtained a job in the field after her graduation but also found time for travel abroad. Of the union between her parents, Lasky writes, "[M]y father could not have found a family more different from his than hers" (29). A practical woman, Hortense refused to marry Marven until he found a steady job. Their courtship spanned 11 years. Remembering her mother's cryptic explanation for the delay—"People thought about things in those days"—Lasky confesses to some curiosity about what else her parents were doing during those interim years (29).

The marriage was apparently worth the wait. Lasky's parents were a devoted couple, celebrating more than 50 anniversaries before Hortense Lasky's death, and Lasky enjoyed their ready affection, as well as a close relationship with Martha. The warm atmosphere in which she grew up has shaped many of the families in her fiction. With only a few exceptions, most of them in her YA novels, the parents Lasky depicts are wise and supportive, the children secure and happy. Typically, when problems arise the family is able to resolve them through shared experiences and conversations leavened with humor.

Marven's bottling and distribution venture proved highly successful, and he and Hortense were able to indulge their daughters in many ways. They spent summers at the family's lake cottage in northern Indiana and escaped to Florida during the harsh midwestern winters. Lasky suffered from childhood allergies, and her parents hoped to cure her runny nose with extended doses of Florida sunshine. Like the twins in her Starbuck Adventure series, Lasky and her sister did not attend school regularly during these months. Her parents believed that "family vacations were just as valuable as school, and they went to great extremes to protect what they felt was an inalienable right in terms of [their children's] education" (AC, 33). So the girls brought work from school and were tutored by their mother, who had imparted a love of literature to her daughters by reading to them regularly. During these extended vacations, Lasky read voraciously on her own. As she and Martha grew older, they also spent part of their summers at private girls' camps.

Lasky acknowledges that her childhood was privileged but is careful to distinguish between being indulged and being spoiled. She learned early that her privileges carried with them certain responsibilities. "Always there were standards, expectations, and values," she has said (AC, 33). These values, including an active concern for those less fortunate and an obligation to speak out on their behalf, emerge repeatedly in her fiction.

Despite her happy family life, young Kathy found Indianapolis less than satisfactory. Like many children, she thought her hometown was "the most boring place in the world," and school failed to engage her. Although she loved the stories her mother told her and, later, the books she read on her own, she was so indifferent to her school's basal texts that her teachers labeled her a "reluctant" reader. "I didn't like the kind of books they had me reading at school—the 'See Dick, See Jane' books," she says. She escaped the tedium through her imagination, inventing stories and nurturing dreams of becoming a writer. "I had been seduced hopelessly by that art," she admits, "first as a reader and then as a secret writer and spinner of tales that I showed to no one."[3] But she regarded a writer's profession as not quite authentic: It seemed "funny" to think of being one's own boss, a situation that sounded "enjoyable" but unreliable.[4]

She credits her mother with encouraging her ambition. In an anecdote often recounted in biographical sketches of Lasky, she recalls a summer night of her childhood when she and her family were riding home from an A&W root beer stand to their cottage. She was sitting in the back of the family's Chevy convertible with Martha, her head flung back, searching the night sky for the Big Dipper. "There weren't any stars," she says. "You could barely see the moon through the thick clouds, and they were the strangest texture, just like wool. I said, 'It looks like a sheepback sky,' and my mom turned to me and said, 'You should be a writer.' "

Although her mother's suggestion was prophetic, Lasky took a circuitous route to fulfilling it. School continued to be disappointing, and her performance there hardly suggested the award-winning author she was to become. "I wasn't a particularly great student," she admits. Although now noted for her engaging children's books on various facets of nature, she remembers her education in the natural sciences with particular distaste. "School did nothing, absolutely nothing, to foster my interest," she says. "I don't know exactly what they did to turn me off, but—ugh." She wrinkles her nose at the recollection. "I guess I got fascinated with the natural world on my own, just by reading and schlepping around with my husband and his camera, seeing what was there and getting excited about it. And not to sound too schmaltzy, but I found that there is a poetry to it, a more profound spiritualism than I ever experienced in organized religion."

Eventually Lasky's parents curtailed the family's long Florida vacations and enrolled her in Tudor Hall, a private Indianapolis girls' school, headed by a stern Episcopal Scotswoman whom Lasky has described as "knowing as much about kids as Mae West knew about Sanskrit" (AC, 34). The atmosphere was restrictive and grim. "It pained them to praise you. At most a teacher might say to my mother, 'She has a way with words,' but they would never tell me I could write well."[5] She was one of only a few Jewish students among the Protestant majority, and at times during chapel, while singing praise to the Father, Son, and Holy Ghost, Lasky crossed her fingers, looked heavenward, and waited for a bolt of lightening to strike her dead. Her YA novel *Pageant* draws heavily on her experiences during those years.

The school had an impressive record for getting its graduates into prestigious schools, but Lasky maintains that "I didn't learn a damn thing except the Lord's Prayer while I was there" (*AC*, 35). Despite this disclaimer, she remembers her French instructor with special fondness, as a "great" teacher, and Mme. Henri of *Pageant* is modeled on her. Lasky has retained some proficiency with the language: many of her young adult characters speak and write in French, and she herself was able to understand people when her research took her to Madagascar, a French-speaking country.

After finishing high school in 1962, Lasky majored in English at the University of Michigan, graduating in 1966. Her memories of her college years are less than fond. "Neither my sister nor I enjoyed college much," she says, "perhaps because we were so happy at home." After graduation, she taught as a substitute in Indianapolis for what remained of the spring term, then toured Europe for several months.

Career Beginnings

When Lasky returned to the States, she set out for New York City. It was the spring of 1967, and her dream of becoming a writer seemed within reach. She hoped to join the staff of the *New Yorker*, imagining that her adroit contributions, however modest, would earn her recognition and the "big chance." But the *New Yorker* had no openings, and she wound up at *Town and Country*. A child of the sixties and shaped, too, by her family's progressive social values, she found herself a "walking anachronism" at the magazine, which is devoted to social events and fashion. With humorous disdain, she writes of working with editors who had "names like Muffy and Bambi and Lacy," enough Pucci dresses for every day of the week, and "barely discernible brain waves" (*AC*, 35).

Kathy in Florida, age five
Courtesy Kathryn Lasky

The experience was not without its benefits, however. She did learn to write jaunty copy—and even gained some inadvertent experience writing fiction under the guise of reportage. Assigned to write an article on the fashion philosophy of 10 New York City women whom *Town and Country* had designated as "best dressed," she interviewed each one over the phone and found them "unbelievably inarticulate and stupid" (*AC*, 35). With a deadline to meet, she just gave up and instead invented a philoso-

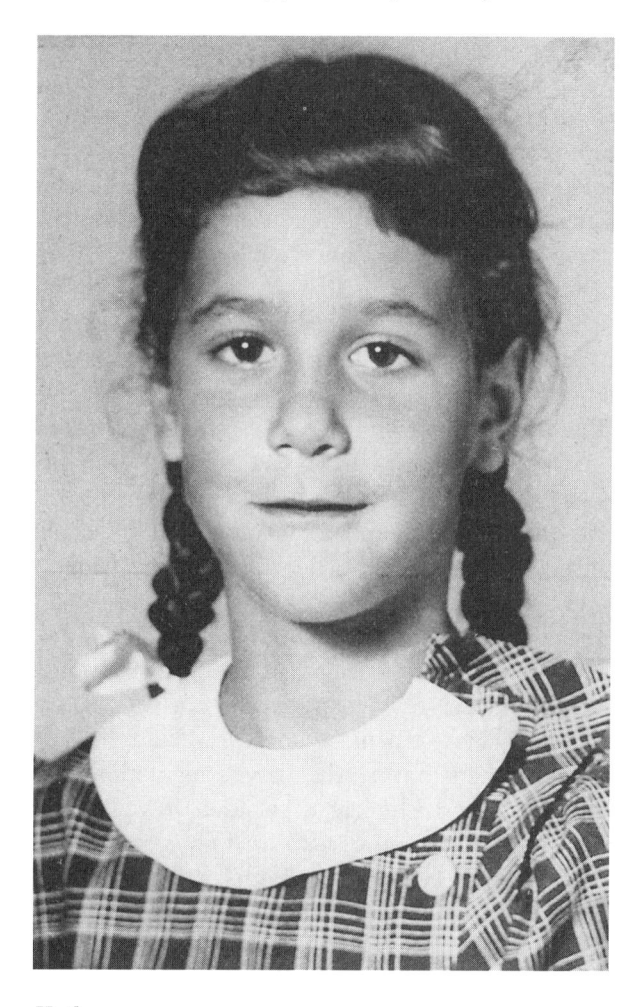

Kathy, age seven
Courtesy Kathryn Lasky

phy for each person, rationalizing that "it would be to their benefit." This same impatience with empty-headed, self-indulgent wealth surfaces repeatedly in her adolescent and adult fiction. Rich, socially prominent characters are often intellectually and morally deficient, with little respect for the natural world, and Lasky portrays them and their milieu with barbed irony.

Inevitably, after a few months she parted company with *Town and Country*. She then gravitated to Cambridge, Massachusetts, where she had many friends, and enrolled as a part-time student in the Harvard Divinity School. She was more attracted to its curriculum of philosophy, literature, and history—all subjects she enjoyed—than to what she and her friends called the "Div Biz," but her studies provided a convenient holding action while she sorted out what she wanted to do next.

While at Harvard, Lasky met Christopher Knight, a graduate student in the Harvard School of Design who also worked as a photographer. Knight first heard of Lasky when a mutual friend, Holly Drew, told him that "this girl with a wonderful personality was moving to Boston" and encouraged Knight to call her.[6] But Knight remembered the lingo of his undergraduate days at Dartmouth. "When someone described a girl as having 'a wonderful personality,' " he explains, "that meant there wasn't much to say about how she looked. So I never called." Then, months later, he took a ski trip with his parents and Holly's family. "When we were out on the slopes one day," he says, smiling at the memory, "I saw this girl skiing. She was really cute, a good skier. She looked great." She was the girl he had refused to contact, and her name was Kathryn Lasky.

After they met and chatted that day, Knight finally made the phone call. Only later did he learn that the two young women had plotted to arrange the meeting because they were planning what Knight calls "some crazy project in Peru" and needed a photographer. But he was going to Romania on a *National Geographic* assignment, and the Peru project never materialized. However, a romance between Knight and the girl with the wonderful personality did.

New Directions

Knight's family tree, solidly rooted in New England on both sides, had produced architects and physicians with Harvard degrees. The paternal side had also produced an assortment of salty types: coopers, shipwrights, and mariners. Knight spent his summers at the family's summer residence on Deer Isle in Maine, developing

Chris and Kathy in Maine, on the occasion of their engagement
Courtesy Kathryn Lasky

a passion for the sea and adventure. By the time he and Lasky met, he had paddled a kayak along the formidable southeastern coast of Alaska from Skagway to Seattle, down the entire Danube river, and through the inland sea of Japan.

In some ways the contrasts between the couple's respective backgrounds were as sharp as the ones between Lasky's parents, but their courtship was much shorter—only three years. They were married on Deer Isle on May 30, 1971, and spent their honeymoon island-hopping off the Maine coast aboard a 30-foot ketch that Lasky's parents had given them as a wedding gift. They christened the vessel *Leucothea* after a mythical seagull in the *Odyssey* whose veil saved Odysseus from drowning in distant seas. The name proved apt, for in future years *Leucothea* was to keep Lasky and her husband afloat through many fierce storms and gale-force winds far from home.

In their first year of marriage Lasky and Knight lived in a Cambridge apartment outside of Boston that Lasky dismisses as a "real dump." Then the couple bought a waterfront brownstone in east Boston; they occupied the top two floors and rented out the other apartments. The brownstone, which they still own as rental property, might be the next stop for a reader searching for Kathryn Lasky Knight. It appears in her YA novel *Prank* as the home of Birdie, the story's protagonist. Birdie's dreams of material success are fed by the building's harbor view of upscale neighborhoods across the bay, and her brother Timmy finds life-changing work on one of the tugboats that ply the waters there.

Not long after moving into the brownstone, Lasky and Knight struck an agreement—what Lasky calls the "bargain in the sky"—that was to provide her with material for future books. At the time, however, three thousand feet above the Maine coast in a single-engine Piper Cherokee piloted by her husband, writing and publishing were far from her mind.

Chris Knight had learned to fly when he was at Harvard, during a breakup in the couple's relationship. Although the split lasted only three weeks, Lasky confides that Knight was "so upset that he felt he had to focus on something else, treat himself to something he had always wanted to do. So he took flying lessons and later got his own plane."

The plane, which Knight playfully called Fly-by-Knight Airlines, provided a handy mode of transportation between the couple's Boston apartment and the vacation home belonging to Knight's parents on Deer Isle. However, the trips were no laughing matter to Lasky. To her skeptical eye, the plane looked like a cereal-box toy, and she envisioned it plummeting into the sea, carrying her to a watery grave. Aware of his wife's trepidation, Chris Knight offered her an alternative: he would give up flying if she would sail to Europe and back on *Leucothea*. Lasky quickly weighed the "beautiful simplicity of ropes, wind, Dacron, three thousand pounds of lead in the keel" against the gravity-defying device that looked like a toy. "It's a deal!" she said (*AC*, 17).

Atlantic Circle

Preparing for the "deal" took two years. The couple set off from Boston in 1974 to begin their journey to England across the North Atlantic. More than once during the monthlong crossing, as *Leucothea* dipped and bounced in stormy seas, Lasky doubted the wisdom of the bargain she had so willingly struck. There was, however, a definite plus: The Knights had agreed to leave *Leucothea* in Europe for three years, returning each summer to explore the fjords and canals of the continent. The first two summers, marked by breathtaking scenery and visits to picturesque villages, proved nearly idyllic. Lasky had begun to work as a freelance writer and she was regularly contributing articles to *Sail* magazine about these experiences.

She had also enrolled at Boston's Wheelock College to earn a master's degree in reading, and each September, when she returned home, she resumed her studies. She describes this step as a "backup" career plan: "Being a freelancer was all very exotic, but standing around with lance poised and not being engaged in 'battle' is always a real fear" (*AC*, 109).

Her graduate studies underscored what her own experiences had already taught her years earlier: that children learn to read from real books, not basal readers. She decided to create a book for young children to read on their own, one with a limited vocabulary but an engaging story and "plenty of white on the page." The result was her first children's book, *I Have Four Names for My Grandfather,* published in 1976. Narrated in the voice of a small child, it tells of the close relationship between the child and his grandfather. "It was really about my own dad," Lasky says. The photographs of the child and grandfather that illustrate the book, shot mostly in the backyard of the Laskys' Indiana home, are by Christopher Knight; the book was the first of the couple's many joint projects.

Lasky also collaborated with her husband on her second book, *Tugboats Never Sleep.* Inspired by the harbor view from the living room window of the couple's brownstone, *Tugboats* also uses a child narrator, who describes in simple but lyrical prose his fascination with the tugboats in the Boston harbor. A closing line of the book, which describes the child's waking thoughts at dawn, simulates his language in the vivid imagery that critics have often praised in Lasky's work: "The northwest wind blows my ears full of soft whistles."[7]

Lasky was excited about the photo essay form that blended her text with her husband's photographs. When the couple began their collaborations, Knight had already gained professional experience with a camera through his work as a photographer for *National Geographic.* However, because the writers and photographers at the magazine worked independently of each other, the photographs often depicted scenes to which the text made no reference, and he was dissatisfied with the magazine's failure to integrate text and image. He also disliked the constant travel his job entailed. And although he had earned a graduate degree in architecture from Harvard, he had little interest in a profession that tethered him to a desk all day. In 1969 he founded his own enterprise, the New Film Company, and began making documentary films just as cinema verité was gaining popularity. When Lasky conceived the ideas for *I Have Four Names for My Grandfather* and *Tugboats Never Sleep,* she wanted to adapt the documentary techniques of cinema verité to create photo books about children. She also decided to publish under her maiden name; she had been married such a short time, she reasoned, that most people she had known over the years would fail to recognize her by any other.

Lasky's father, Marven, is the grandfather in the photographs of the first book; the child is Lasky's nephew. The little boy in *Tugboats* is the son of a college friend. "We didn't have any children yet," Lasky explains, since the couple had postponed having a family until their Atlantic adventure had come full circle. They had yet to bring *Leucothea* home.

For this, the final leg of their adventure, they planned a journey of five months, down the east coast of Spain and back across the Atlantic to the Caribbean island of Grenada. Although Knight had promised his wife that the return route across the southern Atlantic would be "a piece of cake," it proved for Lasky to be as exhausting and frightening as the first crossing. They were plagued from the outset by walls of icy wind and rain, against which "*Leucothea* staggered like a dazed contender in the ring with a heavyweight champion" (*AC,* 166). Lasky longed for the comforts of home—a real bed, friends, movies, the *New York Times.* She and her husband had been married for five years now. Was it for this that they had postponed having children?

After a bout of particularly unpleasant weather, Lasky, desperate and angry, made herself clear: She wanted a more stable life, both literally and figuratively. She was not asking for a snug house in a monochromatic suburb, only journeys of a somewhat different nature. "I had never considered myself anything but a voyager," Lasky maintains, but she didn't consider a boat a sine qua non ingredient (*AC,* 168).

Lasky has recounted her experiences at sea in *Atlantic Circle,* a lively and wry account of the couple's adventures and misadventures. She published the book under Kathryn Lasky Knight, the name she continues to use on all her books for adults to separate them from her books for children and young adults. Philip S. Weld, in a preface to *Atlantic Circle,* describes the work as a "subversive harpoon of a book" (*AC,* 9). Indeed, Lasky's sardonic tone punctures the mythical romance of sailing while also conveying the sense of wonder that the voyage inspired. She moves from blunt comments on hygiene at sea—29 days without a shower—to lyrical passages on the pleasures of people and places encountered. Reviewers gave the book high marks. Writing for the

Library Journal, Susan Ebershoff-Coles praised the book as "witty, funny, and serious."[8] *New York Times* reviewer Christopher Buckley agreed: "[This is] a thoroughly engaging, funny, and beautifully written book," he said.[9]

Lasky's Atlantic circle bore additional literary fruit 20 years later when she was asked to contribute to Scholastic's Dear America series, historical novels aimed at middle-school readers. Each book is rendered as a diary by a young girl living through a significant event in American history. Lasky was allowed to select her subject, and she was delighted to learn that no one had yet claimed the *Mayflower* crossing. "I knew for a fact that no one could match me in terms of conviction and authenticity in writing the sea stuff," she says. "I know Atlantic gales inside and out. I have thrown up, puked, caste [vomited] at almost every longitude between Boston and Land's End in England."[10] The protagonist she created, Remember Patience Whipple, whose story is titled *A Journey to the New World,* does the same on the *Mayflower.*

Parenthood

When the Knights returned to Boston, their Atlantic circle complete, they began the journey into parenthood that they had postponed for so long. Almost a year to the day after landing in Grenada, in December of 1977, Lasky gave birth to her son, Max, named after the little boy in Maurice Sendak's *Where the Wild Things Are.* Five years later, in August 1982, she gave birth to her daughter, Meribah, named after two ancestors on her husband's side of the family. The original Meribah was abducted by Indians and became the wife of a chief. "Hence little Meribah," Lasky says (*AC,* 19).

Lasky had always liked the name Meribah. When she was pregnant the first time, she intended to use it if she had a daughter. When told after Max was born that she would probably have no more children, she decided to use the name Meribah for the protagonist of *Beyond the Divide,* her second young adult novel. She found out she was pregnant again the day she finished it, and when a daughter was born, she regretted having given away her favorite name. Her husband, however, reasoned that since the other Meribah was "only make-believe," they could use the name again. Lasky thought about his argument for "about two seconds" before agreeing. So Meribah Lasky shares her name with Meribah Simon of *Beyond the Divide*.

Today, Lasky and Knight limit their sailing to Maine's Penobscot Bay, and *Leucothea* is anchored at their Deer Isle home. The home and the ketch are the logical next stop in the search for Kathryn Lasky Knight, for both continue to play a significant role in Lasky's life and work. Lasky defers questions about the ketch to her husband. "He's the one who waxes ecstatic," she says, and she is right. Asked to comment on *Leucothea,* he responds, "How many days do you have?" A genial man whose ruddy complexion and keen gaze testify to his avocation on the water, he explains with pride that *Leucothea* is "a Herreshoff" (a reference to a famed English yacht designer) with a lot of teakwood and a self-steering mechanism, then adds—on a fond note—that she is "sea kindly." He does all the maintenance work on her, hauling her out of the water for the winter on a contraption that Lasky describes as "something you might use to move a pyramid."

Their island home, which they purchased in 1985, is an early-nineteenth-century farmhouse of weathered gray shingles nestled in a bay on Northwest Harbor. Lasky, whose hobbies include gardening, has taken advantage of the sunny lot to plant colorful flower gardens, which surround the back porch overlooking the bay. Knight has lit the gardens for night viewing. "It's like sitting in the middle of a bouquet," Lasky says. She and her family spend most of their summers on the island, some of it sailing *Leucothea* on extended trips around the bay.

Lasky's Children's Fiction

Many of Lasky's children's stories are set on Maine islands or the New England coast. In each, as in Lasky's young adult fiction, the protagonist becomes more independent and self-confident through experiences that comprise the plot. *My Island Grand-*

mother, dedicated to Lasky's mother-in-law ("the original Island Grandma"), follows young Abbey on a summer visit to her grandmother's island cottage. Abbey learns to swim and sail and, like many of Lasky's young adult protagonists, takes an active interest in the constellations. *Jem's Island,* dedicated to Chris Knight ("Paddler of a thousand miles"), tells how the boy Jem plans, with his father's guidance, a kayak trip from the family's summer home on Deer Isle to an island of Jem's choosing. The father in the story tells Jem of his own kayaking adventures, which closely parallel Knight's risky trip down the Alaskan shore. As father and son chart and then undertake their journey, the reader learns much about kayaking and navigation. This is a story about growing up, about the need for a child to strike out on his own and for parents to let go at the appropriate time, themes that are repeated in Lasky's YA fiction, particularly *Pageant.*

Fourth of July Bear, as its title suggests, also develops the theme of independence. Rebecca leaves her city home and her friend Emily with great reluctance, unhappy about her family's plans for a summer island vacation. But she learns that new friends are to be found in the close-knit island community and that it offers pleasures to rival the more familiar ones of the city. Sam of the YA novel *Home Free* is also diffident about leaving a familiar environment but learns, like Rebecca, that new places can bring unexpected friendships and satisfying challenges.

The setting for *Sea Swan* moves to the Massachusetts coast north of Boston. It is an unusual children's book in that its narrative viewpoint is not a child's but a grandmother's. Several publishers rejected the book on those grounds before Macmillan accepted it, but the book has proved popular. Readers of all ages can relate to its theme of independence and the need for challenging, engaging experiences. The book takes its title from the small house that grandmother Elzibah, 75 and widowed, builds on the coast after she learns to swim. She has always been cared for by her family and servants, and her move marks her first time being alone. In her solitude, however, she is not lonely. Almost all of Lasky's YA protagonists undertake a similar journey toward autonomy, what Sashie of *The Night Journey* calls being "apart."

Sea Swan looks ahead to Lasky's adult novel *The Widow of Oz*, about a widow who, like Elzibah, purchases a seafront cottage, where she develops a renewed—or new—sense of self.

Lasky's Early Nonfiction

Lasky's knowledge of ships and sailing prompted her first nonfiction work, *Tall Ships*, about the imposing clipper ships of the nineteenth century. The book traces their history and the implications of their sometimes dubious cargoes of opium and slaves. It also conveys a colorful picture of the men who sailed them, many of them young boys longing for a seagoing adventure. Some of its illustrations are taken from pictures and photographs in Maine museums and private collections; others are photographs by Christopher Knight.

Working on this book, Lasky discovered the place of imagination in nonfiction. She had compiled all the necessary facts about her subject, having spent a summer in Salem's Peabody Museum. Still, she could not understand the lure of the sea for young boys in the nineteenth century, particularly in light of her own discomfiting Atlantic crossings: "Why 14-year-old [boys] would give their eyeteeth to sail on ship seemed beyond me."[11] Then she read that historian Samuel Eliot Morrison had said that history is one-tenth fact and nine-tenths imagination. "I started imagining," Lasky explains. "That meant forgetting who I was and the fact that while I was crossing the Atlantic Ocean I would rather have been in Bloomingdale's. I had to imagine what it would have been like to be 14 in the year 1856 in a one-street town in Salem" ("Reflections," 531).

Unlike Sergeant Joe Friday on the old television show *Dragnet*, who wanted "just the facts," Lasky goes beyond the facts in her nonfiction to seek, as she says, "a nonfactual kind of truth that focuses on certain aesthetic and psychological realities" ("Reflections," 532). Perhaps it is this approach that allows her to move easily as a writer between genres. For her, the boundary between fiction and nonfiction is flexible, even elastic. A nonfiction project may lead to a novel. Or her research for a novel may produce a work of nonfiction. Says Denise Perry Donavin, "Not many writers can cross genres and age levels with such aplomb."[12] She often has several works in progress at the same time, both fiction and nonfiction, some on related subjects or with related themes. "I get on these kicks," she says. Much of her work combines fiction and nonfiction: informational books may include imaginary scenes, and her fiction brims with information. Ideas crowd her mind. "My writing," she says, "does me before I do it" (537).

She has never been plagued with writer's block, a happy circumstance owing not only to her unquenchable curiosity about the world but to writing practices she developed when Max was very young. As a new mother, she was "overwhelmed" by how one small baby consumed so much of her day. "I often thought, What did I do with my time before I had children?" Having to make the most of her limited time, she sandwiched her writing into brief but efficient intervals while Max napped. The habits she developed then still serve her well. "I think about the books I'm going to write for vast periods before I actually begin them," she says, "so they're already very worked out before I write a single word."

When Max was about 18 months old, she sent him to a play group three mornings a week. By then, the Knights had found city living less than ideal for raising a child and had moved from their brownstone to a home in Newton, a Boston suburb. A reader searching for Kathryn Lasky Knight might choose to skip this stop. It was, Lasky says, "a boring house in a boring neighborhood," exactly the monochromatic suburb that she had disavowed during her blowout on *Leucothea*. The Knights lived in it less than a year. Nonetheless, it was in this house that Lasky began to write regularly. With Max gone nine hours each week, the young mother found herself with "acres of time."

Lasky had wondered if she could write anything longer than 32 pages, the standard length for children's picture books, and with more time available to her felt challenged to try. She chose as the subject a family anecdote that her aunt Anna had told many times about escaping from czarist Russia to America. The result was to be *The Night Journey*, Lasky's first YA novel. While Max was at his play group, she wrote steadily in longhand on pads of yellow legal paper; each afternoon, while he napped, she typed what she had written.

At this point in her career, with only a handful of publications to her credit, she was hardly an established writer, but she had developed a vision of the writing she wanted to do—writing that combined a strong narrative line with the fascinating information she discovered in her research. She was well on her way to fulfilling the prediction that her mother had made so many years earlier.

Kathy at work in her study
Chris Knight

2. Searching for Kathryn Lasky: The Writer

In 1980 the Knights moved back to Cambridge, into a brown shingled three-story Victorian house built in 1891 by a nephew of Ralph Waldo Emerson. They continue to live here, in a neighborhood of curving streets and stately old houses, only a few blocks from the Harvard campus. William James once lived around the corner, and the large gray clapboard house next door formerly belonged to e. e. cummings. It is a far cry from the "dump" of their first Cambridge residence.

Lasky's Home

The yard is deeply shaded, and Lasky has created leafy gardens of hostas, ferns, ivy, sweet woodruff, and European ginger, accentuated with beds of colorful impatiens. A brick path winds through the greenery to circle the house. Lasky admires Oriental gardens, and her landscape design has touches of them. Boulders from Boston's north shore highlight one corner; a spill of flat, gray rocks covers the ground in another. But Lasky's tastes are eclectic. In the backyard, a cherub perches on the edge of a fountain, holding a fish that spouts water. The cherub once belonged to Lasky's parents, and she has placed him within view of her kitchen window.

This house should be a major stop for readers in search of Kathryn Lasky Knight. It appears in her fiction as the home of Calista Jacobs, the protagonist of Lasky's mystery series for adults. It is stately but not pretentious, "cool by nature with its high plaster ceilings and triumvirate of venerable trees."[1] Inside, traditional elegance is coupled with whimsy and generous splashes of color. An occasional wall is sponge painted deep red or green, accenting the colors of the Oriental rugs that warm most of the rooms. Seascapes hang over tables and fireplaces, and family photographs cluster on tabletops and bookcases and walls, even the walls of the guest bathroom.

A major point of interest, of course, is Lasky's study. It is located to the left of the wide entry hall, across the landing—two steps up and two steps down—of a graceful stairway that climbs to the second floor, each of its spindles carved in a slightly different pattern. The study is cozy, crowded with books and photographs, strewn with papers and souvenirs. On the floor are file boxes set at haphazard angles. Chris Knight affectionately calls the room "a disaster area." Lasky only shrugs, smiling. "I hate housework," she says.

A curious visitor could browse here for hours. Overhead is a brass Art Deco light fixture that blossoms into pink glass shades. Lasky likes to shop during her travels, and she found this fixture in New Orleans while attending a conference. A large table to the right holds Lasky's computer and printer as well as piles of folders and sheaves of paper; yellow Post-it notes border the computer monitor, each with a cryptic notation. The wall behind the desk, sponge painted in deep reds, is hung with art Max and Meribah created as children.

To the left is a large bay window. Framed by deep bookcases, it looks out on a forsythia in the front yard. Award certificates are scattered on the shelf in the bay window. "Oh, those," says Lasky. She means to frame or file them—someday. Lining the adjoining wall are floor-to-ceiling bookcases, full to overflowing, crowded with books and family photographs: Max and Meribah at various ages, Meribah (a serious dance student) in ballet poses, parents and siblings from both sides of the family, Chris Knight smiling into the camera—all testaments to the value Lasky places on family life. Marriage and children, she says, "have made me a better person."

Posters of book covers—*True North* and *She's Wearing a Dead Bird on Her Head*—are propped on the floor against the bookcases. There are fragments of dinosaur bones in a shallow bowl and an old wagon wheel hub by the fireplace opposite the window, souvenirs of Lasky's research trips out West. A hand puppet of Miss Piggy, all curls and long eyelashes, dangles from a lamp next to the fireplace.

The cardboard file boxes hold what Lasky calls "stuff," the residue of completed books and the seeds of future ones: reviews, speeches, research notes, airline and hotel reservations, outlines. Lasky outlines her books before beginning to write, then revises the outlines as she works her way through a project. She may produce as many as 18 outlines for one book. There is a separate box for each book, its "stuff" filed in labeled folders. Some boxes are slated for storage in an upstairs room; others have already been carted there.

Milestones

Photographs and books. Books and photographs. This is exactly the kind of room that a reader of Kathryn Lasky's work might imagine. It was here that she finished *The Night Journey,* published in 1981. That year also marked two other milestones for her, the publication of *The Weaver's Gift* and *Dollmaker: The Eyelight and the Shadow,* the first two of her four children's books on traditional crafts, all illustrated with Knight's photographs. The weaver's gift of the first title is a blanket for Max, a toddler when Lasky wrote the story; he appears in the closing pages. The book conveys a strong portrait of the artisan who raises the sheep and creates the blanket. This book, like *Dollmaker* and Lasky's other two craft books—*Sugaring Time* and *Puppeteer*—focuses on the human side of her subject, on the creative problems an artisan must solve. The dollmaker must translate her understanding of muscular and skeletal structure into the face of a doll that matches, with photographic exactitude, its human subject. The family making maple syrup must know exactly when to draw the boiling sap from large vats into buckets. The puppeteer, working alone on a production of Aladdin, must devise a way to move across a small stage 40 slaves leading 40 camels leading 40 elephants.

Lasky draws her artisans as fully as any fictional character; the reader shares the tensions of their circumstances as each grapples with the dilemmas at hand. Lasky uses this problem-solution structure often in her informational books, populating them with intriguing people, then setting up and resolving problems to create a plot. This approach generates a forward movement and interest often reserved for fiction.

Lasky dismisses the notion that in nonfiction there is no need for characterization or mood, and she develops both effectively. Her craft books, infused with a warm, personal style, were groundbreaking. "Who had ever heard of a voice in nonfiction?" Lasky asks. She rejects the notion that nonfiction should be primarily concerned with "facts first of all." To this commonly held concept Lasky retorts, "I do not believe that a satisfying experience in literature derives from knowing all the facts. This condition suggests to me a kind of mechanical mystery, a sort of soulless exploration of . . . an almost totally explainable and knowable world" ("Reflections," 529).

Lasky's nonfiction demonstrates her conviction that facts cannot explain everything. In her descriptions of the artisans at work on their various crafts, she portrays a mysterious joining of the human spirit with the tools of a trade. Whether spinning and weaving, producing maple syrup, making puppets, or creating lifelike dolls, each of these artisans expresses a unique art that is "a mystery, a miracle that has to do with talent but that is beyond explanation" ("Reflections," 529).

Lasky's craft books earned strong reviews and several awards. *The Weaver's Gift, Puppeteer,* and *Sugaring Time* were designated ALA Notable Books. *Weaver's Gift* won the Boston Globe–Horn Book Award for Nonfiction, and *Sugaring Time* became a Newbery Honor Book, one of the highest distinctions in children's literature. Almost all reviews noted Knight's "abundant" and "beautiful" photographs that illustrate the books.

What Jane F. Cullinane, writing in the *School Library Journal*, says about *Sugaring Time* has been echoed by other critics about all four craft books: "The photos and text combine to make this a rare kind of nonfiction, informative yet as easily read as fiction."[2] The acclaim culminated in 1986, when the *Washington Post* awarded its prestigious Children's Book Guild Nonfiction Award to Lasky for the body of her work.

She is careful to give her nonfiction what she calls "plenty of breathing space," generous white margins that contrast with the format of other, textually denser photo essays. She finds the format of her collaborations with Knight "dynamic," a distinct contrast to the drab nonfiction books available to her as a child, of which she read very few.

Lasky and Knight take great pride in their joint projects. "We get along great," Lasky says, unable to recall any friction in their professional cooperation. Lasky describes their collaborative projects as something between *National Geographic* and cinema verité. Knight aims for the photographic quality of the former but never poses his subjects, thus achieving the spontaneity of the latter. Text and photographs combine to create what one reviewer called a "you are there quality."[3] The couple are very selective about what they undertake, choosing only those projects that offer the potential for what Lasky calls "the perfect meshing of text and images."

Usually it is Lasky who conceives the idea for a project and writes the proposal. However, the result is collaborative in all respects: as she and Knight work through each project, Knight's photographs shape the final book as much as her text does. He designs the layout for each page, making rough sketches of his pictures and matching Lasky's text to them, suggesting additions or deletions. Meredith Charpentier, who edited many of Lasky's early books, characterizes their collaboration as "absolute": "From Chris I always got very specific materials, very specific dimensions. From Kathy I got a very imaginative text."[4]

Some of the Knights' photo essays feature both children. Max and Meribah (affectionately called Beba by her parents) made their first joint appearance in *A Baby for Max,* a picture book that follows the final days of Lasky's second pregnancy, the trip to the hospital, and Meribah's homecoming. Although Lasky is credited for the text, Max is the actual author. He dictated his impressions of each day's events to his father, and Knight's photographs capture Max's sometimes enchanted, sometimes dubious response to the newcomer.

In addition to the photo essays, Lasky undertook another novel for adolescents, and in 1982 she published *Beyond the Divide,* historical fiction about a young woman who travels with a wagon train on the Oregon Trail. Its many characters and shifting narrative viewpoint set a pattern for Lasky's future historical novels, which all examine complex moral issues rising from specific events in the past and include abundant information about their respective times.

The range and depth of information in Lasky's work, both nonfiction and fiction, is impressive, representing a staunch commitment to time-consuming, meticulous research. "I love doing research," she says. "It's so much fun, like a treasure hunt." However, she claims that she retains little of the information she uncovers in her research: "I learn it only for while I'm writing the book. I love it and I love to read about all this stuff, but I don't have a very retentive memory." Still, she can recover the "stuff" when necessary. "I have an almost photographic memory of where I've read things in books," she says. "I can go back to a book I've read six or eight years ago and find within a short time—less than an hour—the exact page and paragraph I'm looking for."

Digging for Facts and Dinosaurs

Preparing to write her next historical novel, *The Bone Wars,* whose plot involves the rivalry for dinosaur fossils among nineteenth-century paleontologists, Lasky traveled to Montana, where she wanted to walk the battlefield of Little Big Horn for a scene in the novel. Once there, however, she realized that she also needed to do some research on other matters, some as basic as "what a dinosaur bone looked like." She had first become interested in paleontology in the second year of her marriage when she accompanied her husband on a trip to Nevada, where he was filming an excavation of an ancient Indian cave. She was supposed to do the sound work for him but describes herself as a "horrible" sound person, so engrossed by the archaeologists' work and so enthralled by the setting that she often let the tape run out: "I'd hang my feet over the ledge of the cave and see these guys digging great things out of the ground. I loved being there. I always thought I'd like to write an archaeological mystery." Eventually she did—but many years and many books later.

Meanwhile, she was committed to *The Bone Wars*, and through a friend she arranged to accompany eminent paleontologist Keith Rigby on a dig to Montana with a group of his students. She took Max along. "We had a blast," she says. "All of this was feeding into my novel, but I told Max, 'We have to come back next year with Dad and Meribah and do nonfiction on this.'" The following summer, the Knight family did exactly that. The trip not only helped her complete *The Bone Wars* but led to two nonfiction works: *Traces of Life* and *Dinosaur Dig*. Lasky refers to these three books as her "bone trilogy"; all explore paleontology, each in a different way.

Traces of Life presents the history of paleoanthropology and examines current evolutionary theory. It takes an unusual approach to nonfiction by combining facts about paleoanthropology and evolutionary theory with fictional prehistoric scenes: a cave artist prepares to paint, a Neanderthal girl shrinks from predators, a family forages for food. Such scenes, together with the book's black-and-white drawings, help readers understand that these early men and women harbored emotions and impulses not so foreign to our own. At the same time, the scientific material remains authoritative and credible. A closing chapter takes the reader two million years into the future to the island of California, where Professor Olcott is teaching a class on Pre-Continental Rift Ancestors. Homo sapiens has evolved into Homo telepathicus, a species that is able—like the twins of Lasky's Starbuck mystery series—to communicate telepathically.

Most reviewers perceived the mix of fact and fiction as a "bonus." "Authoritative and highly readable," said Ellen Mandel, writing for *Booklist*.[5] "[A] shining example of what science books can be," added Jon R. Luoma in the *New York Times Book Review*. "In the end, what should make this gracefully written book a model for books on scientific topics is its capacity for generating goose pimples."[6] Predictably, however, a few critics remained skeptical. While Betsy Hearne, writing in the *Bulletin of the Center for Children's Books,* admired many aspects of the book, she felt that "the least helpful aspects of the book are the simulations, such as the description of a young Neanderthal girl's nightmarish fear of predators . . . or the futuristic holographic/telegraphic lecture by a 'Pacific Rift University' professor in the year 2,001,988."[7] Similarly, *School Library Journal* objected to Lasky's "intermingling of fiction and nonfiction."[8]

Dinosaur Dig returns to the subject of paleontology, taking a different but equally unconventional approach. Illustrated by Knight's photographs, it chronicles the family's expedition to Montana while informing the reader about dinosaurs and the methods scientists use to search for fossils. The emphasis is on the human side of the expedition—the rigors of scrambling over steep buttes of eroding strata, the discomfort of digging beneath the scorching Montana sun, the wonder of touching a newly excavated bone. The awe that Lasky voices at the moment the bone is uncovered might well be expressed by Thad of *The Bone Wars*: "[T]his is the first sunlight that has touched these bones, buried for 67 million years. . . . She [Lasky] has made a connection with a time she barely believed existed."[9]

Many reviewers, such as Cathryn Camper in *School Library Journal,* liked Lasky's unusual strategy: "While most dinosaur books for children concentrate on the dinosaurs, Lasky focuses on the techniques used to recover the bones, presenting the potentially confusing science of fossil recovery as both an intriguing and an understandable art."[10] Reviewers who balked at the unconventional approach objected mostly to its narrative emphasis on the Knights. The *New York Times Book Review* voiced the most frequent criticism, that "outsiders may be less than enchanted by the book's focus on family life in a Badlands paleontology camp, rather than on the dinosaurs themselves."[11] Whether readers are engaged by Lasky's innovations or prefer their information straight, both *Traces of Life* and *Dinosaur Dig* helped to redefine nonfiction books for children, opening the door to imagination in a world that is, as Lasky says, "a very complicated place" ("Reflections," 532).

More Young Adult Fiction

In the years between *The Bone Wars* and *Traces of Life,* Lasky published three young adult novels: *Prank, Home Free,* and *Pageant.* All are set in the present, and each traces a strong-willed protagonist through a coming-of-age progression, a pattern common in YA fiction. "I love writing for adolescents," Lasky says. "I feel the same vulnerability that they feel. When I was young, my mother used to say, 'Don't believe people who tell you that this is the best time of your life. It isn't. It's the worst.' Kids are trying to define themselves, find out who they are. I can connect pretty well with that feeling."

Although all three of these novels use the rite-of-passage structure typical of most stories about contemporary adolescents, their young protagonists mature through atypical experiences, focusing more on social issues than on appearance and popularity. Each novel includes, in characteristic Lasky fashion, information on a wide range of subjects: historical facts about nineteenth-century child labor abuses and the Holocaust, literary interpretations of Tennyson's "Idylls of the King," scientific details about eagles.

More Children's Fiction

As Meribah and Max grew older and Lasky found more time to write, her list of publications grew. Many of these later books were illustrated stories for children. Lasky seeks specific qualities in an illustrator, always hoping for an artist "who adds something." She may make recommendations, but the final choice is the publisher's. Although she has occasionally been dissatisfied with the results, more often she is gratified by what her stories gain through the illustrations. She points to *She's Wearing a Dead Bird on Her Head* as a happy example. Originally skeptical about combining David Catrow's cartoonish pictures with her text, in the end she was delighted with the humorous dimension they added.

Many of Lasky's picture books share with her young adult novels a thematic focus on the importance of having friends, meeting challenges, and respecting nature. The child narrators of *I Have an Aunt on Marlborough Street* and *Pond Year,* like many of Lasky's YA protagonists, are sensitive to their immediate environs and enjoy them in the company of a special companion. Grace, the child narrator of *Solo* and *The Tantrum,* confronts seemingly daunting trials but learns from coping with them; determined and spunky, she might well be a younger version of *Pageant*'s Sarah Benjamin. *The Gates of the Wind* and *Cloud Eyes* take a turn toward fantasy, yet—like some of Lasky's YA fiction—they yield a pragmatic "truth" about the value of living in harmony with the natural world. She has created a contemporary myth in each of these books. In *Hercules: The Man, the Myth, the Hero,* Lasky delves into classical mythology to explore the story of Zeus' mighty son.

More Nonfiction

Lasky's respect for the natural world has continued to generate nonfiction books, all collaborations with her husband. Like their predecessors, the more recent books weave a strong narrative line through abundant fact to heighten interest in people and places. Her research for these projects has carried her across national boundaries and oceans, and readers in search of Kathryn Lasky Knight should have a suitcase handy to follow in her footsteps to Iceland, Florida, Alaska, Mexico, Belize, Madagascar, and England.

Surtsey: The Newest Place on Earth, an ALA Notable Book, describes the formation of an island off the Icelandic coast. So compelling are the descriptions of its ecological evolution that one reviewer found "the book . . . hard to put down."[12] Into her scientific explanations, Lasky wove passages from the creation myth of *The Prose Edda*, a Norse epic. The result is what Roger Sutton in the *Bulletin of the Center for Children's Books* calls "a poetic and intriguing synthesis that reveals the stubborn hold of science and myth." In the same review he describes Knight's dramatic photographs as "National Geographic gorgeous."[13] When Sam of *Home Free* travels back to the beginning of time, the scene before him might well be the emerging Surtsey.

Some of Lasky's nonfiction about the natural world centers on a scientist or naturalist, much as her craft books focus on an artisan. In *Think like an Eagle*, a direct outgrowth of Lasky's research for her YA novel *Home Free*, she and Knight follow veteran wildlife photographer Jack Swedberg through a cycle of seasons as his work carries him to Florida, Massachusetts, and Alaska. Lasky's text, illustrated with photographs by Swedberg and Knight, is both lyrical and succinct. While conveying the demands of Swedberg's profession, the book also delivers fascinating facts about animal behavior and their natural settings. As Ellen Fader noted in *School Library Journal*, "Readers will come away with a sense of awe for the natural world."[14] The shots of Massachusetts' Quabbin Reservoir serve almost as a visual epilogue to *Home Free*, and its information about eagles connects directly to the novel.

Monarchs, a Parents' Choice Silver Medal winner, describes the life cycle of monarch butterflies and their migrations to winter habitats in California and Mexico, usually by butterflies too young to have made the journey north. Again, Lasky's family travels with her, but the focus remains on the butterflies, whose mysterious migrations and increasingly problematic survival create the narrative suspense. In portraying the people active in preserving the conditions necessary for the monarchs' survival, Lasky crosses cultural as well as geographic boundaries to explore some of Mexico's natural wonders and customs, a move that foreshadows her growing intercultural interests. Reviewers gave this book unqualified high marks: "There is much to learn, enjoy, and ponder in this beautiful book," said Margaret A. Bush in the *Horn Book*.[15]

"Vibrant description melds with fascinating full-color photographs in a book that strikes a perfect balance between science and humanity," said Susan Oliver in *School Library Journal*.[16]

When Lasky and her husband traveled to Mexico as part of their research for *Monarchs*, they discovered the subject and title of their next collaboration: Days of the Dead, a Mexican holiday in late October. On this holiday, people honor the spirits of deceased relatives and friends by marking their graves with flowers and setting out tables laden with their favorite foods to welcome the departed spirits home. Lasky's book emphasizes the celebratory quality of the holiday: it is a time for warm memories, not mourning. She weaves information about Days of the Dead into the story of one Mexican family as they observe the rituals. This was the first of Lasky's books to move entirely outside her own culture, and it does so with sensitivity. Reviewers commended her "eloquent" and "vivid" text and Knight's "dramatic" photographs.[17]

Lasky was so taken with the celebratory nature of the holiday that she adapted some of its rituals to mark the anniversary of her mother's death. "My mother had an enormous influence on me," Lasky says wistfully. "Since her death, I somehow feel deprived." Rather than light a single commemorative *Yahrzeit* candle, as prescribed by conventional Jewish observance, Lasky makes an *ofrenda*, an offering to her mother, setting out many candles, flowers, and some of her mother's favorite possessions, mostly books. Then she and Knight toast the memories of her mother with a Manhattan, her mother's favorite drink.

For *The Most Beautiful Roof in the World: Exploring the Rainforest Canopy*, Lasky and Knight traveled farther south, into Central America. At the heart of the book is naturalist Meg Lowman as she explores the rain-forest canopy of Belize. Again, reviewers praised Lasky's ability to describe scenes and relate facts that are, as *Booklist* said in a starred review, "vivid and memorable."[18] Although Lasky and Knight accompanied Meg Lowman, they are not part of the story, but the book dedication hints at the rigors of her research: "[T]he author of this book would like to express her heartfelt thanks to all the people ... who helped her make the ascent into the canopy despite her fear of heights."[19]

Lasky acknowledges that climbing into the canopy was an ordeal, although it was less terrifying than her earlier experiences hiking into the Grand Canyon. "At least in the canopy the greenery is so thick that there's the illusion of something under you," she says. "I was okay when I was still, so I just tried to get from one platform to another. The worst parts were climbing the ladders and crossing on those swinging bridges. Chris was just the opposite, climbing to the ends of every branch and swinging out from the platforms." Knight praises his wife for undertaking this project. "Heights don't bother me," he says, "but she was scared. The person who's scared of something but does it anyway has a lot of courage. She was the brave one." Lasky smiles wryly, and her smile confirms the challenge of the adventure and the teeth-gritting "bravery" that her husband has described.

Lasky's most recent nonfiction book for children, *Shadows in the Dawn: The Lemurs of Madagascar*, took her to the island formally known as Malagasy, off the east coast of Africa. There, she and Knight, accompanied by Meribah and the family of Knight's brother, joined primatologist Allison Jolly to study the island's 30 different species of lemurs. This slender volume (only 62 pages, many of them given entirely to Knight's stunning wildlife photographs) is packed with fascinating information about Madagascar, Jolly's work, and—most especially—the ways of lemurs. The close observations of Jolly and her students in chapters titled "Leonardo's Troops" and "Spite and Death" introduce readers to the methodologies of primatologists while also drawing them into the lives of these primates—their personalities, their conflicts, their triumphs and losses. When tensions between two troops cause the death of a baby lemur, Lasky conveys a genuine sense of the mother's grief in crisp, objective prose that is unexpectedly moving.

Mysteries

Lasky also has tried her hand at writing mysteries, completing two series in the genre: the four Calista Jacobs mysteries for adults and the three Starbuck twins adventures for middle-school readers.

Both series are set in contemporary times. Reviewers sometimes designate the Calista Jacobs mysteries as "YA" or recommend them as "adult books for young adults," perhaps because Calista has a teenage son who plays a major role in each novel and because bookstores often shelve the Starbuck adventures, which feature 12-year-old twins, with its young adult fiction. However, the Calista Jacobs series, with its lusty adult protagonist, is clearly adult fare, and the Starbuck series is more appropriate for middle-school readers.

Lasky's venture into mystery was motivated by her decision to write fiction for a mature audience. "Children's literature is looked upon as a stepchild of literature," she says, "and I felt I had to prove that I could write a novel for adults." A mystery seemed a good starting point. She liked "the comfort of the framework," a problem-solution structure that echoes the pattern she used with her craft books. "You start out with a problem," she says, "and it has to have a beginning, a middle, and an end. It's really clear cut."

Also, she had read some mysteries she describes as "really bad" (Donavin, 247) and thought she could do better. And she was drawn to the possibility of crossbreeding mystery with a comedy of manners, one of her favorite genres. A fan of Jane Austen's novels, she liked "all the social criticism in them—all that stuff about manners and money." She had already developed a bent for social satire in her contemporary YA novels, which poke sardonic fun at such foibles as fashion fads, urban sprawl, religious fundamentalism, and gender stereotyping. In the Calista Jacobs series, she has taken aim at cults, intellectual pomposity, and snobbery, particularly of the Boston Brahmin variety.

Calista Jacobs has much in common with her creator. Calista, too, hails from Indiana and has the same thick, unruly hair streaked with silver and shored up with the same "industrial-strength barrette" that Lasky uses. She lives in a house whose description matches that of Lasky's house and is raising a son much like Max: he is personable, smart, interested in science, and expert with computers. Calista is also professionally involved with children's books, but as an illustrator rather than a writer. Like Lasky, she is irreverent and straightforward, espouses some of the same causes, and displays the same impatience with pretense.

Two of the Calista Jacobs mysteries thematically parallel two of Lasky's YA novels. The first in the series, *Trace Elements*, provides a twentieth-century commentary on the historical subject of *The Bone Wars*, the scurrilous tactics paleontologists use to best each other's research. The book begins with the seemingly accidental death of Calista's husband and concludes with the discovery of the plot behind his murder. Much of it unfolds in the Southwest, the setting that Lasky had envisioned years earlier as "the perfect venue for an adult mystery." *Mortal Words*, like Lasky's YA novel *Memoirs of a Bookbat*, targets the religious right, expressing some of the same negative views of its leaders as bigoted and hypocritical moralists.

The remaining two novels, *Mumbo Jumbo* and *Dark Swan*, are equally merciless in their satire, exposing, respectively, the chicanery behind New Age cults and the shameful secrets of a snobbish Brahmin Boston family. Most reviewers gave this series high marks. *Booklist* called *Trace Elements* an "accomplished novel . . . uninhibited by the stereotypical characters and formulaic action that so often typify the genre."[20] One critic, however, objected to the book's "rather elaborately wrought plot" and all the scientific information, and another found Calista, who is indeed outspoken, "rude, scornful of people with tastes different from hers, not a heroine to root for wholeheartedly."[21] *Dark Swan*, the last in the series, earned the most unqualified praise, perhaps because it is, as Denise Perry Donavin said in *Booklist*, a "well-plotted tale, which lacks the scientific and pseudoscientific elements of Knight's earlier novels."[22] *School Library Journal* found the conclusion "riveting," and *Publishers Weekly* observed that "Knight's deft tale is laced with sharp social insight."[23]

Calista's son, Charley, is actively involved in solving all four mysteries, and Calista's observations about him provide a perspective on adolescents that might well be shared by Rachel's parents in *The Night Journey* or Sarah's in *Pageant*:

> Adolescent eyes . . . were not innocent; yet they were far from knowing. Calista had looked hard into the eyes of Charley and those of his friends. When the masks lifted, there was an unsettling mixture of distrust and hope. It was of paramount impor-

tance for kids of this age never to let the hope show through, not even a glimmer. It was bad form to be caught out with hope in your eyes. It was really a balancing act. Of course, that was what all adolescence added up to—an incredible, nerve-racking balancing act. Thank heavens Charley had a sense of humor. For both parent and child, negotiating the shoals and drafts of adolescence without humor would be the absolute pits.[24]

Like his adolescent counterparts in Lasky's YA fiction, Charley is intelligent and reflective, humbly realizing while gazing at the night sky that he is a tiny speck on a very small planet in a minor galaxy (a perception echoed so often and in such similar phrasing in Lasky's novels that it becomes less a motif than a repetition). Charley holds strong ethical convictions, and his moral stamina is matched by unusual physical fortitude. Both are tested when, inching closer to the heart of the mystery and its solution, Charley finds himself in mortal danger. In the best tradition of the genre, he is rescued only at the last minute in cliff-hanging episodes involving a confrontation with the villains.

Despite their harrowing adventures, Charley and Calista remain essentially unchanged by their experiences. Instead, the emphasis in each novel is on plot, on the mystery and the challenges of solving it. Although mother and son move beyond the grief they suffer over the loss of Charley's father, there is little character development in either over the course of events.

G. K. Chesterton once said that anyone who didn't like mystery or detective novels was an anarchist. His comment implies that the plot of these novels advances from a point of chaos to the restoration of order. The detective functions not only as a clever intelligence in piecing together the clues to a solution but as a moral agent who reestablishes some sort of balance. He is able to do so precisely because his personality is fixed or settled. Thus it is not surprising that Lasky's detectives are among her most constant characters. When Calista stumbles into each mystery, she bends unwavering determination and energy on tracking a solution, her concentration focused even in the face of what might send lesser souls running for cover. She can do this because she is free from the kind of internal conflicts that, for example, beset

Sarah Benjamin of *Pageant* or Dorothy of Lasky's adult novel *The Widow of Oz*. Nor does she arrive at their life-altering epiphanies. The personalities of the Starbuck protagonists are similarly fixed. The central characters of this mystery series for middle-school readers are 12-year-old fraternal twins, Liberty and her brother, July, so named for their shared Fourth of July birthday. Their younger sisters, five-year-old Charley and Molly, are also twins, but identical ones. These children seem to have no friends outside their family. They are regularly uprooted by their father's changing jobs and separated from their mother for long weeks at a time, yet they demonstrate no hint of adolescent angst or the loneliness that plagues the protagonists of Lasky's YA novels. In a "family album" appended to the first novel in the trilogy, July explains, "Liberty and I never have to say hello or goodbye because we are always sort of connected, and because of this we never feel truly alone."[25]

The twins can communicate with each other telepathically. The channels are clearest between each set of twins, but all four children can "teleflash" among themselves. The telepathic device provides humor when the children's messages ridicule the follies of adults; it also provides a convenient means of outwitting the villains. Two sets of telepathic twins in the same family are, as the title of the first novel announces, *Double Trouble Squared*, and Lasky herself has described the Starbucks as "wacky."[26]

In contrast to the Calista Jacobs series, these mysteries are about not murder but mayhem, much of it broadly comic, even in the face of some hair-raising episodes at the climax of each. The plot complications depend on improbable, madcap episodes mixed with fantasy, the resolutions on zany coincidence. Lasky has anchored this fiction to serious themes, but most reviews echoed the response of *Publishers Weekly*: "Lasky has created pure adventure with little regard to credibility or character development."[27] However, while noting the "far-fetched" nature of the plotting, reviewers also praised Lasky's vivid descriptions of setting and attention to detail, as in *School Library Journal*'s review of *A Voice in the Wind*: "[Y]oung readers will be drawn into the mystery and the well-researched history of the area. Lasky skillfully weaves together Native American lore and the beauty of the Southwest."[28]

Lasky published the first Starbuck novel in 1991; the other two, *Shadows in the Water* and *A Voice in the Wind,* followed in quick succession, in 1992 and 1993. All use a similar plot structure. In the opening pages, set in the family's Washington, D.C., home, Liberty and July sense a restless voice or spirit summoning them. Their father, Putnam, is between jobs but soon accepts a prestigious position that takes him to intriguing locales: the heart of London, the keys of Florida, the mesas of New Mexico. Their mother, Madeleine, is tethered to her business in Washington, so when Putnam takes the proffered job, he takes along both sets of twins, too. He also engages Zanny the Nanny, the children's favorite baby-sitter and an elementary school teacher who gladly exchanges her classroom students for the Starbuck children. She designs a site-specific course of study for each trip: the English curriculum, the Florida curriculum, the New Mexico curriculum. Lasky visited each site as part of her research for these novels, and the settings, as one expects from Lasky's fiction, are rendered in convincing detail. The reader as well as the twins learn much about each locale and its culture.

When Lasky initially tried to sell these books, publishers balked at their settings. She quotes a letter from one editor to illustrate the "packaging" mentality among publishers that threatens writers' creativity:

> London is just too foreign and so are the Florida Keys. We need more middle America and with that I mean more shopping malls, more McDonald's. We need the children to be having real everyday problems—issues of being popular, clothes, being accepted, peer pressure—even complexion problems. After all, isn't the older set of twins on the brink of puberty? ("Creativity," 707)

This is exactly the kind of fiction that Lasky has avoided, and eventually she found a publisher willing to forego McDonald's for London, Florida, and New Mexico.

Once the twins are settled in each new location, the voice summoning them becomes more insistent, always introducing a mystery with an element of fantasy. To solve each mystery, Liberty and July creep out at night, and the final resolution is preceded by a frightening episode that endangers the twins' lives. The bad guys are very, very bad, caricatures in the Disney mode; they wreak havoc not only on their specific victims but on the social fabric and physical environment of the Starbucks' world. Thus, when the villains are vanquished, the twins are publicly acclaimed as heroes.

The twins occasionally find themselves at odds with their parents, especially their father, but the intergenerational conflicts here, unlike those in Lasky's contemporary YA fiction, are more a source of humor than commentary on parent-child relationships. The twins telecommunicate brassy comments about their parents that are far more impertinent than any expressed by their YA counterparts. Putnam seems the stereotypical dolt of a father, well meaning and accommodating but easily manipulated by his offspring. Despite Putnam's professional intelligence, the reader, too, is likely to find him an amiable fool. He is the only parent that Lasky has cast in such a condescending, though benevolent, light.

Lasky says she receives more mail in response to the Starbuck series than to any of her other books, and it is easy to understand why. Each novel posits circumstances of enormous appeal to young readers, not only the escapades themselves but the unusual quarters in which the twins are lodged with each new move. Their London house, converted from a stable once belonging to Arthur Conan Doyle, is a charming old Victorian structure with a secret attic niche and a friendly ghost. Their Florida home is a houseboat, with a slide leading from their bedroom window into the waters of the lagoon. Their desert home, perched on a mesa with a spectacular desert view, has a ladder instead of a slide. In each case, the twins are able to come and go secretly, usually in the middle of the night. What 10- or 12-year-old would not relish the prospect—at vicarious safe remove—of exploring the backstreets of foggy London, swimming with dolphins under starry Florida skies, galloping on horseback across the mesas of the New Mexican desert? Who would not enjoy the publicity and applause that await the twins at the end of each adventure?

Lasky always has something serious to say in her fiction, and this series, despite its escapist bent, is no exception. *Double Trou-*

ble Squared speculates about the creation of Sherlock Holmes and explores, Pirandello fashion, the relationship between the writer and his characters; it also brims with information about the history of England and British royalty. *Shadows in the Water* addresses the problem of toxic waste and graphically demonstrates, as does *Home Free,* the effects of pollution; in addition, it provides a wealth of details about the physiology and communication of dolphins, much as *Home Free* does about eagles. *A Voice in the Wind* examines the controversy over ownership of ancient Native American artifacts and teaches the reader about the culture of the vanished Anasazis; its narrative is enriched with Indian legends. Issues common to Lasky's fiction—oppression of Native Americans and gender stereotyping, for example—also surface in these novels.

In addition, Liberty and July share certain characteristics with their YA counterparts. They are intelligent, spunky, witty, and adventurous. They respect the rights of animals as well as of humans, believe in just causes, and act on their beliefs. They gaze into the night sky and speculate on their place in the vast universe. And ultimately, they bask in the same morally benign light that Lasky's YA protagonists occupy: they want the best not only for themselves but for their world.

Historical Fiction for Middle-School Readers

In addition to the Starbuck adventures, Lasky has written historical fiction for middle-school readers. Her first novel, *A Journey to the New World: The Diary of Remember Patience Whipple,* is part of Scholastic's Dear America series, whose books use diary entries as a narrative device, giving readers a sense of everyday life during eventful times in American history from the perspective of young girls. Remember's story is of the *Mayflower* crossing and the early years of Plimouth settlement. Lasky followed this novel with a second for the series, *Dreams in the Golden Country: The Diary of Zipporah Feldman, a Jewish Immigrant Girl,* about a young Russian immigrant growing up on the Lower East Side of

New York City at the turn of the century. The Dear America books have enjoyed an enthusiastic reception, winning the Jefferson Cup Award for the best American historical fiction series of 1996. Scholastic is publishing a parallel series for young male readers, My Name Is America, and Lasky is working on a novel about the explorers Lewis and Clark for this project.

Scholastic has also called upon Lasky to contribute to yet another series, this one on a variety of princesses both famous and obscure. The subject of her first novel for this collection will be the young Elizabeth I, and Lasky plans to write a second on a less well-known princess whose identity is not yet determined.

Lasky's historical fiction for middle-school readers is not limited to books in a series. She has published a novel, *Alice Rose and Sam*, in which Mark Twain—or more accurately, Sam Clemens—plays a major role. Set in nineteenth-century Virginia City, Nevada, it is a blend of mystery, adventure, and social commentary as well as a coming-of-age story and includes what Lasky describes as "some of [Twain's] pithy and most astonishing sayings."[29]

Biographies

Most recently, Lasky has ventured into biography, a move that seems nearly inevitable given her interest in all kinds of people—artisans, scientists, historical figures. Her initial foray into the genre was the improbably titled *She's Wearing a Dead Bird on Her Head*, a picture book that narrates a chapter in the lives of two adult women, Harriet Hemenway and Minna Hall. By founding the Massachusetts Audubon Society, these women spearheaded a movement in the late nineteenth century to protest the popular fashion of decorating women's hats with bird feathers. Often, the feathers were arranged to simulate an actual bird.

At issue was not only the survival of endangered avian species being slaughtered for their plumage but also the status of women. Such ridiculous headgear demeaned the women who were wearing it, and as Lasky says in an author's note at the end of the book, "The bird-hat protest movement became linked in subtle ways with suffrage, the right of voting."[30] Thus, *She's Wearing a Dead Bird on Her Head,* although broadly humorous, conveys two of Lasky's primary concerns: preserving the natural environment and achieving equality for women. Both surface in her YA fiction. The book also typifies Lasky's approach to nonfiction and historical fiction by blending fiction with fact, adding dialogue and incidents that, although probable, are strictly imaginary. (She is careful to separate fact from fancy in her author's note.) The result is an engaging story with two strong main characters. Joanne Schott, writing in *Quill Quire,* might well be addressing many of Lasky's books when she says, "Her account is strongly plotted, suspenseful, and enjoyable."[31]

Lasky followed this book with *The Librarian Who Measured the Earth,* an illustrated story of the life of Eratosthenes, an astronomer in ancient Greece who discovered a way to measure the circumference of our planet. Lasky calls her biographical picture books "portrait biographies." This one begins with Eratosthenes' birth and follows him into old age. Few details of his personal life survive, but Lasky has fleshed out her story by providing information about the schools and libraries of the period as well as explaining in understandable terms complex equations for measuring the earth. She has also tried to fill in the gaps about Eratosthenes by creating scenes that emphasize his insistent curiosity about the world around him, not (as she says in her author's note, which prefaces the book) by making up facts but trying—as she did in *Dead Bird*—"to responsibly imagine based on what we already know."[32] Consequently, Eratosthenes emerges as a three-dimensional individual, "full of character," as one reviewer said.[33] The book, added *School Library Journal,* is "[a] fine combination of history, science, and biography."[34]

Lasky has also written a portrait biography of Mark Twain, *A Brilliant Streak: The Making of Mark Twain.* It follows his early years, before he became famous. That Lasky would write this biography is hardly surprising, given her admiration for Twain. "I love him," she says. "If I could be anyone in history, I'd want to be Mark Twain. I wouldn't have liked the sadness—but the first 30 years were great. He's probably the most moral person I've encountered in history, the greatest American storyteller." She particularly admires him for defying the institutions of his time that condoned slavery. "He began to question authority and slavery, yet he grew up in a family that owned slaves. He was totally irreverent, such a goofball."

Lasky was interested in doing a biography on Sarah Breedlove Walker, an African-American originally from Indianapolis and one of its first women millionaires. Known as Madame Walker, she made her fortune developing hair products for African-Americans. However, when Lasky proposed the idea to a publisher, she was told that "a biography of a black woman written by a white author would be panned by critics and wouldn't sell." Such constraints spelled censorship to Lasky, and she wrote an article for the *New Advocate,* a journal on children's literature, refuting the idea that culturally specific books should be written only by those who come from within that culture.[35]

Suddenly, Lasky found herself in the middle of the culture wars. In the next issue of the journal, Violet J. Harris, a professor who specializes in multicultural literature, rebutted Lasky's position, questioning her ability to create an authentic biography of Madame Walker: "Unless Lasky immerses herself in research, discussions with others, and contact with artifacts, the rhythm of text is likely to be Revlon not Ultra Sheen, *Life* magazine rather than *Ebony* magazine, the milquetoast sounds of Pat Boone rather than the whoops and hollers of Little Richard."[36] Lasky was quick to respond with a letter to the editor, which appeared in the next issue of the *New Advocate.* Although she couched her rejoinder in the restrained language of critical discourse, her disdain for Harris' position was clear. She cited many critics who have written "compellingly" about the "dangers of remaining hostage to the ideology of authenticity" and quoted Henry Louis Gates, W.E.B. Du Bois Professor of Humanities at Harvard, as saying, "No human culture is inaccessible to someone who makes the effort to understand, to learn to inhabit another world." She then deals directly with Harris' comments about her:

> It is regrettable that Harris has elected to attack my writing of a book I have never written.... Implicit in [her] statement is the

assumption that I would fail to research the topic thoroughly. After two decades of writing books for children, including at least half a dozen novels of historical fiction, the one thing I am known for is my thorough and close to impeccable research. It baffles me that Harris suggests that I would now abandon a practice that has been such an integral part of my discipline as a writer.[37]

Lasky seems to have had the final word on the subject, both in print and in life. There were no more exchanges on the subject, and following this incident, another publisher approached her about doing the book, dismissing any objections based on race as "nonsense."

Usually Lasky's response to critics is less heated and more detached. She remains unperturbed by negative reviews. "I don't pay that much attention," she says. "Some of them are off the wall, but these are basically subjective responses, and everyone's entitled to a subjective response." What does exasperate her, however, are inaccurate reviews, in which reviewers confuse one character with another or inadvertently demonstrate that they have read only a fraction of the book. But she is too busy, her life too crowded, to give even this irritation much attention. Other, more significant matters claim her attention and creative energy.

Editors who have worked with Lasky note this singular energy that she brings to her work. Anne Leit of Scholastic, who has worked with Lasky on her Dear America novels, describes her as "dedicated" and praises her "extraordinarily good" research and vivid characters. "She's an agreeable writer to work with," says Leit. "She has very strong feelings about what she's trying to accomplish, yet she's very adaptable, 100 percent willing to make changes, and she goes out of her way to revise for accuracy."[38]

Says Meredith Charpentier, who edited many of Lasky's earlier young adult novels, "It's easy for Kathy to write. She often spills out her story on to the page. I helped her trim it up, crisp it, to make sure it was just as she wanted. I loved her main characters. I always felt that she was Sherlock Holmes and I was Watson. The story was afoot!" Then, after a pause, she adds, "Her stories have dimension, and they are emotionally true. In fact, 'emotionally true' sums up her texts."

3. Toads in the Garden: Kathryn Lasky's Approach to Historical Fiction

When Lasky began to write for young adults, she found much of her material in the pages of history. "I love the past," she says. "The research is neat, sort of like trying on clothes. Some of my contemporary novels also require research, but it's not the same. It doesn't have the exotica." Historical fiction, she says, is her favorite genre in which to write.

Keyhole History

Lasky describes her approach to historical fiction as "keyhole history," which she defines as history rendered from the perspective of ordinary people during extraordinary times. "You press your eye or your ear to the keyhole," she explains, "and listen in. It is not just the great battles. It has as much to do with writing grocery lists, dealing with stomachaches, feeling grumpy and scared to death and mad as hell" ("Keyhole," 6).

Although Lasky makes the "listening in" sound nearly effortless, what she sees and hears through the keyhole evolves from weeks and months, sometimes years, of meticulous research. There is no margin for errors or anachronisms in historical fiction, and Lasky immerses herself in painstaking inquiry before beginning a historical novel, sifting through archives, reading stacks of books about the period, and visiting the site of each setting to envision it as vividly and precisely as possible. The very scope of her research poses a problem of balance: how does an author keep a narrative moving but also communicate the information necessary to bring the period alive? Lasky admits that it is sometimes difficult to control the burgeoning body of information that her research produces. "There's this great temptation," she says. "I've done all this research, and I really want to use it. It's like nine-tenths of an iceberg that's underwater. It supports that tip that shimmers on top, so one way or the other it's there, but it doesn't all need to be there. That's a lesson I've learned over the years." Indeed, her more recent historical fiction is tighter, more focused than her earlier novels.

However, even when submerged beneath the flow of narrative, Lasky's research is hardly wasted. Nor would most writers of historical fiction dispute the necessity of painstaking preparation and scrupulous attention to historical detail. In an article titled "Writing Historical Fiction," literary critic and novelist Thomas Mallon says, "Only through tiny, literal accuracies can the historical novelist achieve the larger truth to which he aspires—namely, an overall feeling of authenticity. It is just like Marianne Moore's famous prescription for the ideal poet: He must stock his imaginary garden with real toads."[1]

Lasky's imaginary gardens abound with metaphorical toads. Reading her historical fiction, readers are not only swept into the lives of her characters but also are introduced to a range of knowledge about each novel's respective period that sometimes borders on the encyclopedic: details about such matters as food, dress, social customs, politics, transportation, and domestic customs.

Accuracy in Historical Fiction

Contradictions in these details with known historical facts can reduce a novel's usefulness or interest, and no serious author of historical fiction takes lightly the matter of accuracy. Writers who work in the genre tell stories on themselves of inadvertent lapses. Author Geoffrey Trease opened his *Mist over Athelney*, set in ninth-century England, with a scene in which the characters sit down for a dinner of rabbit stew. Only after the novel was published did an 11-year-old reader spot a problem: there were no rabbits in England at that time.[2]

Usually a copy editor catches and corrects these kinds of errors, but not always. Lasky herself was tripped up when she allowed a character in *Beyond the Burning Time,* her seventeenth-century novel about the Salem witchcraft trials, to carry a kerosene lantern, which wasn't used until the nineteenth century. She accounts for this anachronistic slip with an interesting autobiographical detail. "I was writing *Beyond the Burning Time* up in our summer place in Maine, where we have kerosene lamps," she said, "and I'm always worried that the kids could set the house on fire. So even though my characters used candles in other scenes, I had kerosene on the brain while I wrote."

The dynamic nature of language poses another problem of accuracy. Vocabularies change from one historical period to another as new words slip into common usage and others become archaic. These transformations impose certain restrictions on dialogue, and writers of historical fiction cannot give their imagination entirely free reign in creating it. The language, of course, must ring true to the character who speaks it, but it must also correspond to the vocabulary of the period.

Several of Lasky's historical novels weave actual historical figures into their cast of characters, an approach that complicates the issue of dialogue. Critic Arthea Reed differentiates between such novels of Lasky's as *The Bone Wars,* which includes not only historic events but historic characters, and *Beyond the Divide,* which includes only the former. She terms works containing historical events "historic fiction" whose purpose is to "reveal history and the true character of historic figures"; works that also contain historic characters she terms "historical fiction" whose purpose is to "bring history to life."[3]

Reed's distinction is useful in suggesting not only the inclusion of actual personages as characters but the extra responsibility that the historical characters place on the author. In developing characters for *Beyond the Divide,* for example, Lasky was constrained only by the necessity to represent the period accurately. In writing *The Bone Wars*, however, she also had to research many of the characters of the period, and the novel offers fascinating glimpses into their lives. The reader learns, for instance, that Custer kept a pet mouse in his inkwell but abused his horse and that "Gary Owen" was his favorite song.

Lasky says that creating dialogue for historic figures poses no problem for her. She has researched them so thoroughly that she feels entirely comfortable putting words in their mouths. In *Alice Rose and Sam*, she even created dialogue for Mark Twain, whose voice is hardly unknown to many readers. Although much of what he says in this novel is drawn from his own work, Lasky's invented speeches weld seamlessly to the famous writer's actual words, perhaps because she identifies so completely with him. In an afterword to the novel that offers a glimpse into the impulse that inspired it, Lasky describes her long relationship with Twain:

> I first encountered Mark Twain many years ago as a young and voracious reader. In our backyard in Indiana there was a pond at the bottom of a hill. I built countless rafts with my best friend and in my imagination I turned that pond into the Mississippi River. What most appealed to me about Mark Twain was that he was a person who had learned all the really important things about life and people in spite of school and in spite of church or organized religion. . . . I loved Mark Twain so much I wanted to be Mark Twain, or, more accurately, I wanted to be Sam Clemens. . . . I had no real desire to be the famous author, but rather the wild boy. There are, however, limitations that have to do with gender and biology. So I thought I would try the next best thing: to become his friend, his dear friend. To accomplish this, I created Alice Rose. She is, I guess, in some sense an alter ego. (*ARS*, 249)

When Lasky's research fails to uncover sufficient information about a historic character to allow her complete confidence in creating his speech and actions, she substitutes a fictional character for the actual one, as she did with some characters in *The Bone Wars*. She then documents the substitution in an appended author's note that explains the historical basis for the character.

When a writer chooses a first-person narrator, the issue of language becomes even more critical. A narrator whose voice relies too heavily on outdated language, however historically correct, is sure to lose readers. On the other hand, a narrator's vocabulary, like the dialogue for all characters in historical fiction, must be restricted to language in use at the time of the story. Authors John and Patricia Beatty tell of finishing their novel *Campion Towers,* set in Massachusetts Bay Colony in 1651. They began to suspect that their young first-person narrator was using some language that did not exist in the 1600s. Although they had carefully researched the period, they now edited their manuscript to trace the history of any questionable words. Their work validated their suspicions: they had to find substitutes for such terms as *mob, aisle, amazing, bewildering, chunk, clunk, carefree,* and *complete* (Glazer and Williams, 363).

Closely related to language accuracy is the issue of narrative voice, shaped not only by word choice but by the narrator's opinions and attitudes. Although Lasky's historical novels for young adults use a third-person narrative viewpoint, they often include first-person mimetic passages such as diary entries or letters that are subject to the same constraints as the voice of a first-person narrator. In addition, her middle-school historical novels for Scholastic's Dear America series are written as diaries and thus require a first-person narrator. Lasky works carefully to create a narrative voice that is authentic, true to the narrator's historical period. "You have to put aside your prejudices," she says. "You have to step back and let your characters speak." She takes care to exclude views that are clearly contemporary, however sympathetic her own viewpoint may be toward them: "I try to be very disciplined, very vigilant, but after I've written 50 or so pages, the voice becomes natural."

Author Joan Blos writes of her decision to cast her historical novel *A Gathering of Days: A New England Girl's Journal* in diary form. This choice allowed her to be "faithful to nineteenth-century New England sensibilities, sensibilities often suppressed by understatement, without boring, alienating, and probably disappointing twentieth-century readers accustomed to books whose protagonists announce their feelings clearly."[4] Having read several authentic diaries to prepare to write the fictional one, she recognized the limitations imposed not only by the first-person viewpoint but by the diary form as well: "For example, dialogue must be used sparingly as diarists tend to report the fact of a conversation, not its word-for-word content. Description would have to be limited to situations, objects, and persons of particular interest to the protagonist herself" (Blos, 279). Blos also notes that the "right" voice not only narrates a given story but "helps to find the story; it leads the story out.... Although the voice is invented by the author, it has its own vitality and is formative as a result" (279–80).

Blos' observations might have been articulated by Lasky herself. The young protagonists of *Journey to the New World: The Diary of Remember Patience Whipple* and *Dreams in the Golden Country: The Diary of Zipporah Feldman, a Jewish Immigrant Girl* disclose thoughts to their diaries that might otherwise remain unarticulated. At one point, for example, Remember makes a list of her "unsettled feelings and worries," reflecting that she does not like the "shadows of fear lurking about." But her list exposes criticism of some adults on the *Mayflower,* which, of course, she would never voice. Instead she writes, "I shall bring them into the light" and confides her feelings to her diary. After writing them, she concludes matter-of-factly, "There be my list of worries."[5]

Zipporah, too, confides her most privates hopes and fears to her diary. She comes to the United States speaking only Yiddish, and the reader is given to understand that the early passages are expressed in her native tongue. However, in her first entry she writes, "I swear on the blessed memory of my grandmother that a year from now I shall be writing in English,"[6] a promise to herself that she fulfills. Italicized text signals the transition into her new language.

Zipporah's voice is distinct from Remember's; it is less restrained and has occasional syntactic deviations that simulate Yiddish. For example, when she learns that her papa, formerly a musician in Russia who has been forced into menial labor to earn a living, has a chance to work again at the profession he loves, she responds: "Oy, I am so excited that I must write in Yiddish. It would be like stuffing the world into a thimble to have to say in English all this excitement" (*Dreams*, 55). These variant constructions sometimes carry over into her English sentences: "There has begun in Russia a little over a week ago a big revolution" (142).

Conforming to Blos' observations about the diary form, the girls' descriptions of events both momentous and inconsequential are limited to circumstances "of particular interest to the protagonist herself," as when Remember describes the moment when she sighted the New World: "We [she and her friend] held each other's hands so tightly and almost dared not breathe, but minute by minute the line [of the horizon] became firmer and began to thicken.... This be the New World and it doth fill my eyes for the first time" (*Journey*, 39). And when Zipporah learns that her friend Mamie has died in a sweatshop fire, she writes, "Death can be over in a matter of seconds for the victim but for the living it is like one long forever streaming with images" (*Dreams*, 146–47).

Blos notes that diaries in general use little dialogue, as do those of Lasky's characters, but Remember's and Zipporah's voices are so strong and convincing that the reader is hardly aware that other voices are missing. And each girl serves, much as Blos describes, to "lead the story out," to determine its direction and shape. Remember is exactly the spunky character, sometimes defiant and sometimes subdued, needed to infuse the old Pilgrim story with fresh interest. Zipporah, the cultural outsider, has much in common with her. Like Remember, she makes new friends, contends with loss, and struggles successfully to make a place for herself in a strange new world. Her story, much of it set in a neighborhood teeming with tenements, touches on issues common to the process of acculturation: generational conflicts, language difficulties, tensions between ethnic groups.

Dreams in the Golden Country was not available for review at the time of this writing, but *Journey to the New World* has been favorably received. Reviewers warmed particularly to Remember. Susan Pine, writing for *School Library Journal*, noted the "observant, spirited" narrator and the effectiveness of her "child's-eye view of the people and events around her."[7] Lynne B. Hawkins praised the "fascinating little tidbits of information which fill out the fiction" and the diary's "appealing heroine."[8]

The Relevance of the Past

Lasky is especially drawn to historical events that demonstrate the intolerance and injustice that have marked (and marred) the chronicles of the United States. Her fiction invariably demonstrates the insistent intrusion of the past on the present, and she is able not only to create vivid accounts of historical events but to address such current issues as racial and religious bigotry, sexual exploitation, gender discrimination, and maneuvers by the powerful to maintain the status quo. Much as fantasy writers create imaginary worlds as a way of commenting upon their audience's actual world, so Lasky's historical fiction works obliquely to disarm readers' resistance to her novels' implications about their own culture.

The young protagonists of Lasky's historical fiction, victims of greed, hatred, and persecution, manage to triumph over their adversaries in the face of incredible odds. Most historical novels for young adults culminate in similar victories. Author Ann Schlee, discussing her own historical fiction, accounts for the prevalence of this pattern:

> In a way, almost all children's books are legends of power and weakness. One has to develop a child character who is, in a sense, a hero with power over the action of the story. Yet, in reality children don't have power in their situations. In the past children were far more exploited, but they also were much more caught up in the web of adult existence. In writing about the past, the writer has the chance to depict [children's] extraordinary adventures and seizures of power.[9]

"Seizures of power" aptly characterizes the central action of Lasky's historical fiction. Her protagonists begin in a position of extreme vulnerability created not only by their youth but also, variously, by race, creed, class, or gender. By confronting their respective circumstances, they assume more control of their lives and gain unanticipated strength and status. This story line, a classic quest archetype, is also popular in contemporary YA novels but, as Schlee notes, lends itself particularly well to historical fiction.

Lasky has pondered the issue of truth in historical fiction, the fine line between historicizing fiction and fictionalizing history. Other writers of historical fiction have also grappled with this problem, for they are necessarily writing about a time and a people from which they are far removed. Does historical fiction reveal more, then, as some critics insist, about its author than about its historical subject? Is it, as Henry Seidel Canby has said, "more likely to register an exact truth about the writer's present than the exact truth of the past"?[10]

Any answer usually stresses the interpretative nature of both history and fiction. Along this line, Jill Paton Walsh contends that more than careful research binds the two. She suggests that history is as much *fict* (Latin for "something made") as *fact* (something done), that while evidence of history exists, it is itself "a construct of the mind."[11] Lasky points to historians' myriad interpretations of "plain history," arguing that they rarely "do it plain" and that no history, whether within a novel or a history text, can be without bias. She distinguishes between writing with a bias and writing with an agenda. "I might write with a bias," she explains, "a bias for telling history from the ordinary point of view, often the female point of view, the nonheroic point of view" ("Keyhole," 8). On the other hand, she says, a writer with an agenda seeks to indoctrinate, and inevitably, agendas distort. She has no tolerance for distortion, even in the name of social benefit and good cause. For example, although her work demonstrates strong feminist leanings, she has expressed concern about frequent portrayals of women so heroic and accomplished that the average reader has little hope of emulating them. "We should not write to set examples," she says.[12] The point of historical fiction is "to educate, to enlighten and never to indoctrinate" ("Keyhole,"

9). She admits that as a novelist, she is probably more "passionate" than some historians, but she shares with them the goal of "truth."

Lasky's truths often counter material that has been sanitized for popular consumption, such as the magnolia-scented romance of plantation life. To this end, she creates characters who challenge the prevailing assumptions of their time, repudiating the moral legitimacy of such precepts as Manifest Destiny or slavery. The protagonists of most YA historical fiction position themselves similarly in relation to the popular thinking of their times, but there is risk in such a pattern. It can result in cardboard characters who function as little more than the writer's mouthpiece. Lasky uses her keyhole approach to avoid this trap. "Literature wherein nobody cries real tears but instead copes with a capital C is literature in which the real fabric of history begins to unravel and become meaningless," she says ("Kitty," 154).

Lasky has been criticized for including some unsavory characters in her historical fiction but insists that "there is room for all of these kinds of women and men in books because they are the stuff of which history is made" ("Kitty," 157). She also defends including actions that may be viewed unfavorably from a contemporary perspective. One reader, after finishing *Beyond the Divide*, wrote to Lasky objecting to the response of some characters to a young woman's rape: they shunned the victim rather than blaming the rapist for the attack. The reader felt that Lasky had not "set a good example" for her young audience (164). Lasky's reply reflects the responsibility she feels to her subject: "Unfortunately, we have a long history of shunning and ostracizing rape victims. As a writer of historical fiction, I have an obligation to remain faithful, to remain accountable in my story telling, to the manners and morals and the practices of a period" (165). On a less formal note, she adds wryly, "They didn't have rape crisis centers back then."

When she spoke to a college class in adolescent literature, several students complained about a scene in *Beyond the Burning Time* in which a hired man hides to watch a woman through a window as she undresses for bed. The students felt that Lasky should provide her young adult readers with examples of "healthy sex" instead of such scenes of "perverted sex." Lasky has little patience with such objections. "Hey," she says, "I didn't invent window peeping."

When an editor at Scholastic Press asked her to write a novel for its Dear America series that would "delve into those moments of quiet dignity" in the life of an ordinary girl growing up in trying times, Lasky wanted to include some "undignified" moments, too. Remembering her own Atlantic crossing, she chose the Pilgrims as her subject and created a protagonist, Remember (or Mem) Patience Whipple, as a fully dimensional child, one with "fits and rages, jealousies, and heartache, good cheer and grumpiness," who knows moments of spontaneous selflessness as well as selfishness ("Keyhole," 6).

Lasky had another goal, too, in writing Mem's story. She wanted to tell of the Pilgrims' crossing and settlement as an immigrant story, to show that they were not necessarily more pure or patriotic than the immigrants who followed in subsequent centuries. Herself the grandchild of immigrants, she chafed at the mythic portrait of morally upright souls who came over on the *Mayflower*. "They were called pilgrims and anyone [who came] after, immigrants. They were considered brave, resourceful, and enchanting. Immigrants were rarely considered any of the above" ("Keyhole," 7). To her delight, her research uncovered the Billington family, a seventeenth-century equivalent of the totally dysfunctional family. The parents were loud and abusive; the children stole. Their presence enlivens Mem's diary and adds to the often-told story of the *Mayflower* crossing a humorous and human dimension. Lasky wants her readers to understand that history has not been made only by heroes and patriots and to see "that ordinary people, people who throw up and get ticked off, played a part, too. And that, most importantly, there is distinction in living an ordinary life with dignity, with hope and with courage" (10).

When Lasky first began to write keyhole history for young adults, she took as her setting the American West of the nineteenth century, a time and place that had long intrigued her. This undertaking later evolved into *Beyond the Divide,* but after a frustrating year of working on the novel, she put the manuscript aside and turned her efforts to another young adult novel whose central action also unfolds in an earlier time but in a very different place.

The Night Journey

This novel was *The Night Journey,* which she published in 1981. Her shortest work of historical fiction, illustrated in black-and-white ink drawings, it provides a bridge between her children's books and her later YA fiction for older adolescents.

The Night Journey actually encompasses many journeys. For this reason, Lasky originally proposed as a title *Night Journeys,* but in 1981 Avi published a book by that same title. Meredith Charpentier, Lasky's editor at Frederick Warne, suggested as alternatives *Time Out of Line, Night Borders, The Adventurers in Time,* and *The Bright Sentries.* None seemed satisfactory. "Oh, damn," Charpentier concluded in a letter to Lasky, *"Night Journeys* was perfection."[13] Finally, Lasky settled on *The Night Journey.*

The title refers most obviously to Nana Sashie's childhood escape from czarist Russia when she and her family fled the pogroms that threatened all Russian Jews early in the century. Lasky based the character of Nana Sashie on an aunt who made a similar journey, and she dedicated the book to her: "For Ann Lasky Smith, who remembers."[14] Nana Sashie relates her story to her great-granddaughter Rachel. Rachel's parents have asked Rachel to spend time conversing with Nana Sashie, who lives with the family. However, they have cautioned their daughter against talking about what they call "the old country," mistakenly fearing that memories from Nana Sashie's past will upset the old woman. Dutifully, Rachel stops by Nana Sashie's room each day and makes desultory conversation with her about the weather and school, topics they both find tedious. Only after Nana Sashie speaks of her own grandparents who were murdered by the soldiers of Czar Nicholas do the two find ground for meaningful communication.[15]

To keep their conversations secret, Rachel sometimes creeps to Nana Sashie's room in the middle of the night, and her surrepti-

Aunt Ann Lasky Smith, the real Nana Sashie
Courtesy Kathryn Lasky

tious visits constitute another night journey, this one back through time and space to the Russian spring of 1900. She hears the story in installments, an episode at a time, and her increasingly mature response signals still a third journey, her own toward adulthood. When she first hears of the horrors inflicted on the Russian Jews, her reaction is sympathetic but self-focused and immature, expressed in the vocabulary of a sheltered 13-year-old whose report card describes her as "unmotivated" and "an underachiever": "She could hardly believe that she was the great-great-great-granddaughter of 'murdered' people. It was sickening. Weird" (*NJ*, 3).

But as Nana Sashie's story unfolds and Rachel comes to know her Russian ancestors, she begins to understand her family better and to value the connections between its generations. In the novel's epilogue, Rachel, now 19 and in college, reflects on the significance of Nana Sashie's story, remembering it as "time out of line, but time laced with the bright filaments of memory that linked two people at the opposite ends of life for a vital moment in each one's existence" (*NJ*, 150). The contrast between Rachel's two responses provides a measure of how far she has traveled from her childhood self.

Nana Sashie's story of poverty and persecution is framed by scenes from Rachel's comfortable life: she has a fight with her best friend, loses a coveted part in the school play, helps celebrate her mother's birthday. Rachel's strand is secondary to Nana Sashie's story, but the juxtaposition of the two lives magnifies the gift of freedom that Rachel's courageous ancestors have bequeathed her. At the same time, it underscores the difficulties of growing up where such freedom is only a far-off dream.

The transitions between the alternating scenes are handled smoothly, often through the repetition of a word or idea that closes one strand of the story and opens another. For example, one chapter in Nana Sashie's story ends with the family's concealing gold pieces in the Purim cookies, or hamantaschen, that they will take on their journey. When Sashie's mother compliments Sashie on how neat, how "perfect" her cookies are, Sashie feels queasy, as if perfection might constitute a threat to the family, calling attention to what they wish to conceal. She then pinches some edges so that they are tight enough to hold the gold but deliberately messy, not "perfect." The next chapter begins with Rachel and her mother planning a costume for Rachel's friend who has been cast in the school play. Rachel chides, "Well, it doesn't have to be so perfect, Mom" (*NJ*, 59).

Reviewers praised the skill with which Lasky moves between Nana Sashie's past and Rachel's present. Peter Kennerley, writing in *School Librarian,* recognized that "the structure of the narrative underlines [a] sense of continuity, and the book is full of images which echo across time and back into Jewish history."[16] *Bulletin of the Center for Children's Books* noted, "The two parts of the story are deftly woven together, with the contemporary scenes having enough humor and characterization to give them substance but not so much that they detract from the drama of Nana Sashie's exciting tale."[17] And a review in *Booklist* by Ilene Cooper commended the way in which the novel's structure helps to sustain its tension: "Just as Rachel must wait to hear the whole adventure, the reader too is tantalized, eager to hear more."[18]

The Night Journey shares much with Lasky's other fiction, both her children's books and her young adult novels that followed. Most notable are the commonalities of characterization and theme. Lasky often creates strong families, and this one is no exception. The adults provide moral guidance to their young, and the occasional friction between generations is eventually resolved in an atmosphere of love and understanding. Family members enjoy each other; they share jokes as well as heartaches, engage in affectionate teasing, and are sensitive to each other's emotional needs. Lasky has genuine empathy for her aging and aged characters: Nana Sashie and Zayde Sol, the two elderly grandparents of this story, are drawn with a warmth and respect that nonetheless make clear the infirmities of age.

The young Sashie of the escape story and the contemporary Rachel typify Lasky's adolescent protagonists in many ways. They are both spunky and creative, ingenious problem solvers undaunted by life's difficulties. Although they are loving daughters, they sometimes grow impatient with their parents; this is especially true of Rachel, who is not above lapsing into the sulky or sassy discourse of American adolescence. Ultimately, however, both Sashie and Rachel rely upon and appreciate their parents' wisdom.

Along with affectionate respect for their parents, both Sashie and Rachel value a growing sense of self and independence from their families. Near the end of Sashie's journey to the Russian border, she wanders off from the family to savor the twilight by herself and finds enormous pleasure in the uncustomary solitude: "This was all so new to Sashie, being outside, watching the sky, feeling the texture of the earth—being apart! It came to her suddenly like a tiny explosion in her brain—being apart, not alone, just apart" (*NJ*, 128). All of Lasky's young protagonists move in this direction, making a place for themselves "apart" but recognizing the need for community. Rachel tells of a similar moment in the novel's epilogue; she has come to her father's office some months after Nana Sashie's death and grieves openly for the first time. When she finally stops, her father says, "Now you can begin, can't you?" (147). The closing pages of the story affirm that indeed she does begin, "apart" from her family at college but lovingly tied to them.

This novel dramatizes two of Lasky's recurring themes: the persecution of those groups whose "differences" arouse suspicion, hatred, and violence, and the seamless continuum of time that carries the past into the present. Rachel's father expresses the first theme when he tries to help his daughter comprehend the Russian pogroms: "People—those in power, the so-called leaders—take a group of people who, because of their looks or practices or beliefs, appear slightly different from the majority.... Gradually they dehumanize these people, make them into abstractions. It's very easy to kill an abstraction" (*NJ*, 10).

However didactic the speech, it serves well to articulate Lasky's concerns about marginalized groups vulnerable to oppression. Here, as elsewhere in Lasky's young adult fiction, language plays a key role in the dehumanizing and abstracting process. The Russians refer to the Jews as Zhidi, a term both derogatory and abstract; like all hate language, it allows the user to demean an entire group without having to identify anyone by name or face. Lasky describes such language as "racist tags that make it easier for nonthinking people to categorize other human beings" (*AC*, 32). Although such language says more about the person using it than about the targeted group, it can serve as a powerful stimulant to violence. In this case, it reinforces the soldiers' view of Jews as subhuman and blunts any sense of remorse, even as they systematically destroy entire Jewish villages.

Lasky enlists the reader's sympathy for Nana Sashie's family without making them so heroic as to defy credibility, creating a cast of Russian Jews—Sashie's family and those who help them escape—who are recognizably human in their shortcomings: keyhole history at its best. They are appropriately courageous and protective of each other, intent on the survival of their people as well as their personal safety, but like most families they sometimes bicker among themselves, their tongues growing sharper as their impatience mounts. Sashie's mother, Ida, expresses her impatience regularly, using rhyming, nonsensical words that capture both her contempt and a Yiddish flavor. When Ghisa says that she can solve the problem of the Purim costumes and adds a suspenseful "But—" Ida retorts, "But schmut! Get to the point" (*NJ*, 28). Her irritation is understandable, for like characters from a Chekhov drama, the adults in Sashie's family often talk at length about changing their lives, but their plans are little more than ineffectual dreams until Sashie suggests a solution that prompts the others to act.

Lasky softens her characters' sharpness with flashes of irreverent humor, expressed mostly in the dialogue. When Sashie's grandfather Zayde Sol urges his family to postpone their escape until after his death, which he believes is imminent, Sashie's Aunt Ghisa retorts, "Why should I believe that you will die imminently—you've never been on time for anything in your life" (*NJ*, 16). Sashie's father, admonishing his family that they must travel light and leave behind their cherished household items, puts his case succinctly: "The idea is to get across the border, not set up housekeeping on it" (32).

Lasky gives her story added dimension by including characters outside of Sashie's family. The most significant of these is Wolf, whose eyes are like "pinpricks of terror" (*NJ*, 35). As his story unfolds, we learn that his family was annihilated when the tsar ordered the destruction of his entire village and that, to his undying shame, he ran away to save his own life, abandoning his wife and child. His haunted appearance terrifies Sashie's mother, who sees him as a devil. So demeaned has he grown that he even appropriates the term *Zhidi* to refer to himself and his people when addressing some Russian soldiers. His tragic circumstances demonstrate the human cost of bigotry while sparing the young Sashie from its extremities. A desperate man with little to lose, he plays a key role in helping Sashie and her family escape, and his efforts restore to him a measure of humanity.

The family intends to flee during Purim, disguised as traveling festival players. As they plan their escape, they recount the biblical story in which Jews were saved from annihilation in ancient Persia through the brave actions of Esther, a Jewish woman, and her cousin Mordecai. Although somewhat digressive, this tale of persecution and survival parallels the experiences of Sashie's family. Together, the two stories emphasize the need to defend one's freedom with unflinching courage. A poem by Simeon Samuel Frug prefacing the book makes clear that survival depends on an indomitable spirit:

> No savior from without can come
> To those that live and are enslaved.
> Their own messiah they must be,
> And play the savior and the saved.
> (*NJ*, n.p.)

Yet the differences between the religious practices of Sashie's and Rachel's families raise questions about the consequences of religious freedom too easily achieved. The Russian Jews live intimately with their religion, celebrating Jewish holidays, preparing Jewish foods, and regularly reciting Hebrew prayers. Isolated from non-Jewish Russians, they speak Yiddish among themselves, reserving Russian for their interactions outside the Jewish community. In contrast, Rachel's family celebrates birthdays; her father decorates his wife's birthday cake with an Eiffel Tower, and he speaks to Rachel in French phrases. Rachel has grown up with little sense of her family's history. Her family seems Jewish more in a gastronomic sense (they enjoy good corned beef) than in a spiritual one. Seen in this light, *The Night Journey* can be read as implying that assimilation poses as grave a threat—if a less violent one—to marginalized cultures as does persecution.

Both Lasky's fiction and nonfiction reveal her great respect for the past, and several incidents in *The Night Journey* illustrate her view of it as a living part of the present. Sometimes the past is transmitted genetically; the three generations of Sashie's family—her mother, her grandmother, and her great-grandmother—look so much alike that Rachel is "caught" by the strong resemblance of the three faces. The story demonstrates, too, that our childhood selves remain with us into old age. As Nana Sashie begins to narrate her story, Rachel observes that she is almost transformed into the young Sashie, the little girl whose tintype sits on the mantel downstairs. Rachel has seen this picture for as long as she can remember, but until now she never thought of the child in the photograph as someone who actually existed. Now, watching her great-grandmother tell about hiding the gold pieces in the hamantaschen, Rachel notices the combination of past and present in Nana Sashie's old memories and youthful gestures, "the slidings back and forth between two realities" (*NJ*, 50).

In a larger sense, the structure of the story itself represents the past and present as a single, unbroken continuum, with the incidents from 1900 injected into Rachel's life late in the twentieth century and the characters from the past looking ahead toward Rachel's present. Nana Sashie tells how her Aunt Ghisa had imagined a future when she showed Sashie a blurry photograph of herself posed between Ghisa and a friend. The photograph, Ghisa prophetically explained, would preserve the memory of the day it was taken and would allow Sashie, growing old in another country, to point to the photograph and say to her children and grandchildren and great-grandchildren, "I was born in Nikolayev!" (*NJ*, 132). It is this picture, we can assume, that sits on the mantel in Rachel's home.[19]

Lasky creates vivid settings, particularly landscapes, and she laughingly claims to have a "landscape gene." The descriptive passages in *The Night Journey,* precise and often lyrical, support her claim. When the young Sashie observes the scene around her family's campsite during their flight, the details are painted in graphic language: "For a few brief seconds the sun on its downwards slip sprayed its light through the island archipelago and drenched the dark mountains in the most glorious rose color. Then the rose seeped out and a cold purple stole over the mountains" (*NJ*, 128). Contributing to the vividly portrayed scenes is Lasky's imagery, often drawn from nature. Rachel observes her great-grandmother holding the initialed tool box that her family took from Russia: "Nana Sashie's fingers, light and quick as hummingbird wings, ran over [her father's] initials, then darted for a sliver of a screwdriver in one of the compartments" (22). As a young girl, Sashie is awed by the sound of a violin played by one of the rescuers, the man she would later marry: "Sashie thought that if butterflies sang, this is the music they would make" (120).

The Night Journey received many favorable reviews for its strong characterizations, its attention to a period of history about which little had been written for young readers, and the skill with which Lasky knit together Sashie's and Rachel's stories to create a seamless narrative. Its excellence earned it an ALA Notable Book designation and the National Jewish Book Award. The smooth narrative flow is interrupted, however, in the epilogue when the novel unexpectedly changes its point of view, shifting from the third person of Rachel's strand to first person, with Rachel herself narrating her experiences following Nana Sashie's death. Lasky says that she used the shift to communicate a movement both in time and in Rachel's development and to create an immediacy not otherwise gained. However, the effect is at first jarring.

A review in the *Horn Book* criticizes the novel's "excessive emotion," and the criticism seems warranted.[20] Occasionally the characters, especially Rachel's architect father, overreact. At one point, for example, Rachel "excitedly" remarks that McDonald's golden arches are copyrighted. That is the extent of her comment, but her father appears to think that his daughter is slipping into a materialistic quagmire: "Rache, does that really impress you—that some guy got his design for these golden arches copyrighted and made a bundle? I mean, is that what you consider achievement? Quality?" (*NJ*, 84). After continuing in this vein, he concludes, "If you think that the greatest thing going in terms of human achievement is some guy who got his design for a hamburger stand copyrighted, I am going to be concerned!" (85).

However, the virtues of the book outweigh these problems. As its critical acclaim has demonstrated, the writerly deftness that Lasky developed in her earlier books for a younger audience is very much in evidence here. Readers fortunate enough to discover the "keyhole" of *The Night Journey* and follow Nana Sashie's escape from the old country will also discover a truth about the value of freedom: that it is a basic human need denied only at great cost to oppressed and oppressor alike.

4. Smelling the Rat: Journeys into the Nineteenth Century

Kathryn Lasky has always been fascinated by American history, and the western frontier of the nineteenth century holds special interest for her. "I have a thing about the old West," she says. "I really wanted to be a cowboy. I almost wish I'd been born then." She admits that as a woman, there would have been "a lot to put up with," but also—most emphatically—"it would have been so interesting. Would I have been a whore? Or a little schoolmarm?" She smiles impishly. "Probably the schoolmarm. But to see this country when it was uninterrupted!" Her landscape gene—as she calls her love of natural vistas, of panoramic scenes and their myriad details—kicks in, and she sighs wistfully. "What a great time! So exciting!"

Although Lasky had long been interested in writing about the old West, she was wary of perpetuating the heroic myths that dominated movies and television. "I've learned to smell a rat," she says about her skepticism toward the romantic stereotypes that obscure the uglier chapters in our nation's history. In search of her rat, she began to read widely about the settling of the West. Her research led her to a book about the last free Indian in North America. She was struck by the appalling toll of the westward movement on not only the Indians but the emigrants, too. The latter suffered terrible hardships during the journey, and many fell victim to the "pernicious greed" for gold that led them to rob and kill each other. Here was her rat.

Kathy hiking out west, collecting images for her western historical fiction
Courtesy Kathryn Lasky

Spurred to learn more, Lasky spent six years doing research before she began writing. Then, only a few chapters into her story, she became stuck and set it aside.[1] Returning to the manuscript after completing *The Night Journey*, she finally published it in 1982 under the title *Beyond the Divide*.

Beyond the Divide

The story centers on 14-year-old Meribah Simon, who in 1849 joins her father, Will, on a wagon train to California during the gold rush. Like Nana Sashie's story, this novel is about a journey, a quest in which the distance traveled is psychological as well as physical. The "divide" of the title refers not only to the geographical site that separates the waters destined for either the Pacific or the Atlantic but to a cusp in Meribah's development when, after a long and difficult struggle, she crosses from childhood to adulthood.

The novel opens late in the story, with Meribah, alone and starving in the mountains that border California, standing over the carcass of a doe and fending off vultures to salvage what food she can. It then flashes back nine months and more than three thousand miles east to the small Amish community of Holly Springs, Pennsylvania, where Meribah is living with her family and where her father is being shunned for attending the funeral of a man who did not adhere strictly to Amish ways. Banished from his own house to live in the barn and unable to borrow money for the seed he needs to farm, Will Simon decides to begin a new life in the West. Meribah chooses to accompany him rather than remain and abide by the stifling rules of the Amish, leaving her siblings and mother behind. The remainder of the novel, whose nearly three hundred pages exceed the conventional length of YA fiction, moves chronologically and reads almost like a journal, despite its third-person viewpoint; each chapter is headed by a notation of time and date that tracks the progress of Meribah's journey. A story of survival in every sense, this novel fairly brims with historical detail, which, while informative and interesting, makes for a slow and sometimes digressive plot. With this book, Lasky has aimed for mature readers who can handle its length and pace.

As is often the case with historical fiction, the setting drives the plot. Initially, it is the rigidity of the Amish community—"the unseen walls, the unvarying measurements, the inflexible proportions"[2]—that propels Meribah and her father westward. Their journey along the Oregon Trail structures the remaining events, creating the rationale for bringing together the diverse personalities that populate the story and providing the physical and spiritual challenges to survival that reveal each of their characters.

Although this is a more complex book than *The Night Journey,* it shares certain features with its predecessor. Like Sashie and Rachel, Meribah is a spirited and intelligent young woman, but more fully drawn, her development closely tied to events along the trail. In Holly Springs her sense of self has been constructed by others; it is concern for what they might say rather than what she herself thinks that constrains her behavior. She has been defined, she realizes, "not by herself but by others" (*BD*, 6). When she leaves Holly Springs, she feels that a deadly weight has lifted, but nonetheless she still depends upon familiar ways for her identity. "We're still Amish, aren't we, Pa?" she asks (23). And continuing to take her cue from what others say about her, she enjoys the glowing adjectives that other emigrants heap upon her, echoing their language to herself although it is far removed from her customary speech: "I'm a lamb, Meribah thought absently, a charming, lovely, delicate lamb" (50).

As the wagon train moves farther and farther from her Amish home, Meribah moves further and further from her Amish ways. Exposed to new people and experiences, her sense of self begins to change. Her fellow emigrants are very different from the people she knew in Holly Springs. Mr. and Mrs. Barker devote much of their time and energy to the enormous store of worldly goods they have brought from Indiana; the Timm brothers, surly and knife wielding, shoot at wildlife and Indians; the affected Billings from Philadelphia, who travel with fringed pillows, throw rugs, and fine china, introduce her to sentimental English poetry and fashionable clothing when Meribah makes close friends with their daughter Serena.[3]

As the journey pushes on, Meribah witnesses acts of greed, destruction, and cruelty that would have been unimaginable to her sheltered, earlier self. The Timm brothers murder two Apache Indians and dangle their scalps from their belts. The path that the wagon train follows is strewn with dead oxen and the graves of cholera victims as well as the wreckage of emigrants who preceded them, most of it tossed from the wagons and deliberately destroyed so that no one else can use or profit from it. By the time the wagon train pushes into the precariously arid territories that border the Rockies, Meribah is torn between the Amish girl that she once was and the young woman she is becoming: "She thought east and looked west. Time and distance mingled oddly, and Meribah wondered about who she had been and who she was becoming and the connection between the two persons" (*BD*, 118).

Events grow more disastrous. Her friend Serena is raped by the Timm brothers, and in the twisted thinking of others in the wagon train, Serena becomes the guilty party rather than the victim. Later Serena wanders off and is killed in a mud slide. Meribah imagines her friend "released in stone" like the fossil of a tiny horse she and Serena had found earlier, a peaceful image that fulfills the meaning of her friend's name but does nothing to assuage Meribah's anger at fate and her fellow travelers. By the time the party crosses the continental divide, Meribah realizes that "she could not look back, and so she turned west. There were no more choices for her" (*BD*, 175).

Her losses mount. Her father injures his hand repairing the wagon of another emigrant, and the wound turns gangrenous. As Meribah assumes more and more responsibility, the distinction between the roles of parent and child blurs; their extraordinary circumstances forge new identities for both Meribah and her father. One of their oxen dies, and when their wagon breaks down on the California border, Will is too ill to repair it. The captain of the wagon train then convinces the others in the group to abandon them.

Meribah meets each disaster with growing determination to survive. She stands up to some of the other emigrants in a manner that earlier she would never have thought possible, even leveling a gun at Serena's father when, as the rest of the wagon train pushes on, he wants to take their wheels for his own wagon. "You'll have to kill me first," she tells him (*BD*, 230). She cuts the skirt off her Amish dress and wears beaver leggings instead, an outer manifestation of her inner changes. Stranded in the mountains with her ill father, she becomes completely self-reliant.

With the death of her father, the story comes full circle to the events of the first chapter. As Meribah sets about making soup from the pieces of the deer carcass she salvaged in the opening episode, a filthy, savage man invades her tent, carrying a knife, and moves to rape her. In a "smooth, almost gentle, gesture" (*BD*,

264), she takes her father's rifle and shoots him point-blank in the face, spattering his blood everywhere. She, who earlier wondered if she could shoot game because handling a gun came unnaturally to her, feels no remorse. Her only concern is for the meat that simmers in the stewpot. "Thank God I put the lid on it," she thinks (265).

Although Meribah has learned that she is physically self-sufficient, she also learns during this period of isolation that she needs human companionship and community. In the closing chapters she is given refuge during the harsh winter by a tribe of Yana Indians, and her friendship with them, especially the woman Meli, stills the ache of loneliness that had gnawed at her, sharp as hunger pangs. In the final pages, she turns her back on California and sets out alone to the east, for the Valley of La Fontenelle, through which the wagon train passed earlier. Her father had brought seeds from Holly Springs and bequeathed them to her before he died, and Meribah wishes to live in a place that will allow her to plant and harvest them. The valley, as she explains to a friend, is exactly such a place. She has learned a new way of living and being, and she is certain that in this valley she can be true to the new self she has become.

Two facets of her story point toward this moment, her mapmaking and her growing empathy for the Indians of the old West.[4] The map of the literal journey that she draws along the way also serves metaphorically to chart her inner voyage. Her mapmaking begins when she cannot make sense of a map her father has purchased and decides to draw her own as she goes, creating a sketch to suggest the "shape of her journey rather than the direction" (*BD,* 41). Her map, then, represents where she has been rather than where she is going, but this is appropriate both literally and symbolically; at the outset she could not have predicted her journey's end or its consequences.

The drawing chalks she purchases in Missouri are for representing nuances rather than the sharp edges of things, a contrast to the precise ink drawings of Mr. Goodnough, a professional mapmaker she meets and whose exacting work represents what she calls "true lines" (*BD,* 35). She would like to emulate his precision so that she might map her soul, for she is beset with "particles of doubt" about her place in the universe. However, she sees too clearly the ambiguities of the world to represent it so unequivocally. She learns much from her mapping, discovering that "every journey [has] several starting points" (43). Her drawings reveal the changing geography of her imagination—both its peaks and its valleys. When she crosses the divide, she makes only a few faint lines, opting instead to mark the Atlantic and Pacific Oceans, neither of which she has seen. With this act, despite her particles of doubt, she has expressed a belief in things she cannot see. This is her father's definition of faith, and he insists it is what makes us human.

Nonetheless, after she crosses the divide, Meribah's faith and vision are diminished by the terrible things she has witnessed, and she limits her perspective to what is immediately before her, no longer trying to capture with her chalks and pencils "the edgeless world and the endless wind" (*BD,* 180). She works only in gray pencil, to match her own dulled state of mind. Nor do her markings communicate anything coherent, because she can make sense of nothing.

Then Mr. and Mrs. Whiting, a couple in the group with whom she has made close friends, become so weakened with dysentery and lung disease that they opt for a double suicide rather than die one at a time along the way, and Meribah stops mapping altogether. As she later explains to Mr. Goodnough, "I just started to wonder where we were moving to" (*BD,* 241). Only much later, when Goodnough leads her and her ill father out of the mountains and she gains a fresh sense of direction, does she take up her drawing chalks again. She creates new symbols to represent what she is seeing, "reinventing" the land, as she later explains to Goodnough, just as she is reinventing herself. His reply reinforces the metaphoric implications of Meribah's drawings: "You are a true mapmaker. Indeed, you map more than you think, Meribah Simon!" (246).

Meribah's growing affinity for the Indians of the American West provides another measure of her development. At first, she accedes to the stereotyped white view of Indians as barbaric. She does not protest when her mother calls her Indian doll a savage, and when Serena's father tells her that the Pawnee are "a terrible thieving lot," she replies, "Murderous, I've heard" (*BD*, 60). But she silently admires the picture of a sleek Pawnee chief and two warriors that she has seen in a painting and is fascinated by their colorful attire. She relates to Indian culture on a more profound level when the wagon train stops at a deserted Pawnee village and she explores an underground earth lodge. Struck by the integrity of its proportions, she feels an empathy for the people who lived there and wonders about their interrupted lives. The repose she finds in the empty lodge stands in sharp contrast to the din and dirt that greet her when she rejoins the wagon train.

She later experiences a similar peace at Fort Hall in the presence of Mrs. Grant, an Iroquois woman whose husband commands the fort. Inside her home, Meribah admires the simplicity of the furnishings. Despite its spareness, she senses a completeness that she finds very satisfying. With Mrs. Grant, she establishes an unspoken bond so comfortable that the "spaces in the conversation were as natural as those in the room" (*BD*, 192). When Meribah leaves, Mrs. Grant gives her a basket of herbal medicines and a pair of beaded moccasins she has made. She also imparts to Meribah a new confidence that helps sustain her during the difficult times ahead, and Meribah senses her presence even after leaving the fort; she is the first of Lasky's characters to communicate telepathically.

One night, when emigrants and Indians camp across a lake from each other, Meribah watches the reflections of both camps in the lake and notes the similarity of the two images. Contrary to the fear, contempt, and hostility with which most emigrants regard the Indians, Meribah sees that a common humanity unites the two races: "The Indian figures and the emigrants were as indistinguishable as the blazing fires" (*BD*, 244). What began as admiration has developed into acceptance of Indian culture. Her stay with the Yana, during which she becomes acculturated into the Indian way of life, completes the process. She observes that this Indian village, like others she has seen along the way, blends seamlessly with its natural surroundings, and she responds wholeheartedly to the Yana way of life, to its simplicity, neatness, and economy. She admires the deft movements of the Indians as they go about their daily tasks and takes pleasure in the orderly arrangement of things in the lodge. Thinking back to Holly Springs, where life was also simple and ordered, she contrasts the two ways of living, noting that in the Indian lodge, the sense of order is maintained not for its own sake but in service to a higher "beauty that was a part of living" (283). The self that emerges after months among the Yana is mature and independent, spiritually attuned to the natural world. She begins to dress like an Indian, in a tunic of shirred bark and grass, and she learns to move like one, scaling rock faces and walking with "muscled grace" and an "easy balance" (292).

So affirming is this transformation that she is now able to accept the hardships and tragedies that have preceded it. When she visits the cave that sheltered her immediately after she killed her assailant, she finds that despite the anguish of those days, an essence of the cave has become part of her. She comes there when, like Sashie on her own journey, she wants to be apart—"alone but not necessarily lonely" (*BD,* 285). Her Yana name is Saltu, meaning "other" or "different," but now she never feels estranged, not singled out as "pee-culiar," the way she was earlier made to feel back in St. Jo when other travelers commented on her Amish dress.

Watching the Yana celebrate the return of spring with music and dance, she thinks back to the particles of doubt that plagued her earlier. Although she still harbors doubts, they no longer torment her. As a final act of reconciliation with her past, she comes to terms with a memory of a "crystalline gray" that has haunted her during her journey. Much as spring has unlocked the frozen earth, her newfound peace releases the buried memory, and she puts a name to the elusive color: " 'Mother,' she whispered. . . . [She] remembered a time long ago and far back, a time of warmth, of fullness, of holding and calm and trust and light, of a voice singing 'Ribah' like the softest lullaby" (*BD,* 287). When she disappears into the distance on the novel's closing page, the effect is poignant, as if a close friend has departed for the unknown. The character of Meribah is so richly portrayed, so fully dimensional, that it is small wonder that Lasky felt she had given Meribah's name to an actual person, not just a child of her imagination.

Meribah's story develops several themes. Concern for the cultural "other" that *The Night Journey* explored is also prominent here. In this case, the Native Americans are the marginalized group, suffering enormous losses: homes, hunting grounds, life itself. The contrast between the filthy and starving Pawnee who come to beg food from the emigrants and the portrait of the sleek warriors Meribah admired earlier bears witness to terrible deprivations. Later, when she visits the deserted earth lodge, she is saddened by its mute testimony to lives whose simple rhythms have been disrupted. Her response parallels the thinking of many contemporary social critics who have commented on the error inherent in talk about "opening" or "settling" the West, as if the original West were unpopulated, unsettled. *Beyond the Divide* makes clear that the wide-open spaces of western myth were places where real people—Sioux, Apaches, Iroquois, Yana—lived and died.

As with the Jews in *Journey*, language plays a significant role in reducing the Indians to the margins of the dominant culture. The whites denigrate the Indians as "savage" and "thieving" while priding themselves on their own "civilization." Meribah is left wondering what civilization actually means. Mr. Billings unwittingly provides a definition after he has been shamed into giving a little of his tobacco and tea to some Pawnees: "So much for civilization. . . . So much for tea and smokes in the starlight" (*BD*, 78), he says, unaware of the irony. But Meribah thinks back to his comment when she visits the Billingses' stuffy tent and feels smothered by all the parlor trappings of pillows and cushions, overwhelmed by cloying smells and smoke from Mr. Billings' tobacco. "So this is civilization," she thinks (89).

As the journey continues, evidence mounts that the emigrants, not the Indians, are the true savages. As Mr. Goodnough says, the hostilities along the way have come not from the Indians but from the white folk, and he adds that if the emigrants continue with their murder and thieving, there will be no one left for the Indians to kill (*BD*, 243). One might argue that Lasky's portrait of the Indians, by dramatizing the gross injustices inflicted upon them, tends to mythologize them and ignore their inevitably human failings (although some are briefly shown as corrupted by the greed of white culture), but the point is clear: it is people's actions, not their race or skin color, that define their "savage" or "civilized" nature.

Concern for the status of women, whose lives are constrained by gender even in the anarchic matrix of emigrant culture, also surfaces in this story. Meribah finds herself exhausted by the end of each day on the trail, yet much of the "women's work" remains to be done: muddy clothes must be washed, damp bedding dried, the cow milked. To compound her weariness, Meribah must help each evening to prepare a "good square meal for the menfolk" (*BD*, 51), as if she had not worked as hard as the males. Serena's rape emphasizes the lack of control that the women exert over their own lives. Prior to her attack, Serena is being groomed for marriage to a fellow traveler, the foppish Englishman Mr. Wickham. Conditioned to think of marriage as her only future, she views him through an adoring haze, and she is offended when Meribah innocently compares Mr. Wickham to Serena's affected father.

Lasky, a fan of Jane Austen's fiction, modeled Mr. Wickham on the equally foppish—and dishonest—Mr. Wickham from *Pride and Prejudice*. Like his literary ancestor, Mr. Wickham's airs conceal a cowardly heart, and when Serena is attacked while strolling with him, he flees the scene, then shoots himself in the foot to pretend an injury sustained in her defense. Once back at the camp, he ignores Serena—as if she had done something shameful. Most other members of the group, men and women alike, follow suit, smugly gossiping about "the incident" or "it" and self-righteously shutting Serena off from the community support she so sorely needs, replicating the shunning practices of the Amish.

These episodes, like others in Lasky's fiction, demonstrate how language constructs each person's version of reality. Serena's name, now heavily ironic, is never spoken after the rape; rather, she is referred to as "she," a "silly flirt," a "tart filly from Philly"; what has happened is not "a *crime committed* but an *incident brought on"* (*BD,* 139). Like the "Zhidi" and "savages," Serena has become nameless and therefore less than human.

This point about language mediating between the external world and each person's perception of it is made again when Captain Griffith, the wagon train master, convinces the others to push on without Meribah and her father. The captain tells Meribah that it is in the best interests of the company to push on, but when he says "best," she thinks "worst." When he says "sensible," Meribah thinks "insane." When the captain refers to the others as "good folks," she retorts that they are not good, that they are murdering her and her father. As the captain continues to argue his case, his language grows more pretentious, his vocabulary more inflated. Meribah notes that he uses big words whenever he is uneasy, especially when his leadership is challenged. The message is clear: through language each of us constructs our own social realities to suit our individual purposes, and language serves handily to obscure what its user chooses not to make clear.

The contrast between the tightly regulated community of the Amish in Holly Springs and the increasingly anarchic community of the wagon train emigrants raises another significant theme, that of individual freedom versus community security. In Holly Springs, inflexible rules governing work, family, and religious beliefs ensure a secure community but allow little individual freedom or spiritual questioning. As a member of the community, Meribah is never plagued with the particles of doubt that dog her once she leaves, but she chafes at the cramped restrictions that, at their extreme, lead to practices such as shunning.

Away from home, however, she sometimes feels lost in the vast West, missing the security of the "fences" that bound her earlier life. And she discovers that freedom exacts its price. Her experiences on the road raise questions without answers, and she is bewildered by the human inclination to destruction that seems to go hand in hand with freedom. Nor can her father, whose wisdom she trusts, explain why people behave as they do. He tells her that there are no answers, only questions. "If thou wants easy answers," he says, "they are in Holly Springs" (*BD,* 157). His reply affirms the value of freedom over community domination.

Still, survival of the human spirit requires a sense of community. After an evening of social dancing around a campfire with the other emigrants, Meribah is comforted, less threatened by the edgeless West. Although she thinks of herself as a tiny speck lost in space, that evening she recognizes that she is also a speck of a larger order. As she learns after her father's death, however physically self-sufficient she becomes, she needs human companionship for spiritual nourishment.

Beyond the Divide includes the compelling descriptions of landscape that enriched *The Night Journey*. Early in Meribah's journey, she sees the prairie as "a strange sea now, liquid and flowing with waves of grass. A stretch of grass caught by an odd wind current would suddenly turn deeper in color and swim away like a school of trout in a clear river" (*BD*, 75). As the heat and rigor of the trip begin to take their toll, the scenery reflects the changes, and Lasky renders the "scorched, parched, and bleached" setting in careful detail (107–8).

Lasky's often unexpected and precise figures of speech also distinguish the style here. Listening to her friend Serena prattle on, Meribah observes that her talk is "laced with curlicues of speech" (*BD*, 37). The procession of wagons and pack animals seems "to ooze in slow undulations across the prairie like a ribbon of molasses, languid but destined" (62). As they move westward, the harsh and rocky country begins to "grind on them like a giant millstone" (100).

Obviously, though, *Beyond the Divide* differs from *The Night Journey* in significant ways. Its multiple issues are more complex, and its greater length permits a wider array of characters and more depth in their development. Its tone is considerably darker, marked by incidents of frank and increasing brutality unrelieved by the family banter and warmth that lightened the earlier work.

Beyond the Divide reflects the same intense and lively interest in a range of subjects that enriches Lasky's children's books of nonfiction. An attentive reader can learn much; there is a wealth of information about Amish customs, United States geography of the mid-nineteenth century, some details of period clothing, the architecture of Indian lodges and western American forts, even the agriculture of figs. Although we might sometimes wish for less detail—in the lengthy discussions of women's fashions, for example—Lasky has managed for the most part to strike an effective balance between information and plotting.

However, one problem does mar the narrative: *Beyond the Divide* shares with *Journey* an unexpected shift of narrative viewpoint. In its closing pages, the story, which has been told from Meribah's tightly controlled viewpoint in the third person, suddenly moves to Goodnough's. The shift does allow us an objective view of Meribah as she, like the speaker in Robert Frost's poem, chooses the road less traveled and disappears into the distance, but it is sudden and somewhat disorienting. A footnote to Lasky's research for this novel may help explain it. The historical counterpart of Goodnough's character, a mapmaker named J. Goldsborough Bruff, kept extensive journals that were published in a limited edition. Lasky obtained a copy during her research and used the material extensively in developing her story (*BD,* 296). In that way, then, Goodnough's (or rather, Bruff's) perspective contributes to the entire story, and his integrity of spirit, his resistance to the corrupting power of greed, provides a significant contrast to the behavior of other emigrants. However, Goodnough has been offstage, so to speak, much of the time, and his viewpoint is introduced so late in the story that the shift seems contrived and intrusive.

Most reviewers concentrated on the many strengths of the novel, which was designated an ALA Best Book for Young Adults and a *New York Times* Notable Book. A review by Natalie Babbitt in the *New York Times Book Review* is typical of critics' reactions: "The result of the author's careful research is a very effective historical novel. . . . *Beyond the Divide* is engrossing, a strong presentation of what life surely must have been like for those amazing souls who crossed this vast country in its unsettled state."[5] Kenneth Donelson and Alleen Pace Nilsen, discussing YA historical fiction in *Literature for Today's Young Adults,* describe the novel as "remarkable," "engrossing," and "surehanded throughout." The less favorable comments focused on the number and nature of the secondary characters. *Bulletin of the Center for*

Children's Books, while describing the novel as "vivid and stirring," noted that the numerous characters "shift the focus from the protagonist."[6] *Voice of Youth Advocates* insisted that "it is not appealing to read about mean, sordid characters like those who people this book."[7] Such criticism seems to miss the point and to ignore the purpose and one of the strengths of this rich and absorbing story: Lasky has written a painstakingly researched novel that requires a scope of characters to portray the westward movement. It was never intended to be a cliff-hanging, shoot-'em-up western with clear delineations between good and bad guys.

Like historians of recent decades, Lasky, too, has stripped the romance from the lingering myth of the American West. Through an engrossing story whose details are almost documentary in their credibility, she has helped readers understand the high cost of expanding the frontier.

The Bone Wars

Lasky's next historical novel, *The Bone Wars,* was published in 1988. Like *Beyond the Divide,* it is set in the American West of the nineteenth century, but a few decades later, during the 1870s. Its story includes two adolescent protagonists, Thaddeus (Thad) Longworth, an American, and his aristocratic English counterpart, Julian DeMott.

A prologue, set in Texas, opens the novel. Thad, five years old, has been asleep under his mother's bed. He is too young to comprehend what awakens him, to understand that his mother, a prostitute, is being murdered by a customer. From his hiding place, he can smell and hear her attacker, a buffalo hunter. Then he sees his mother's hand dangling over the bedside, the fingers torn and bloody. The graphic scene leaves its mark: Thad is struck mute by the trauma and does not speak for two years.

The story then jumps ahead nine years. Thad, now 14 and still trying to forget the awful moment, has been working in a saloon mopping floors. One day he is hired by a kindly cattle herder, Mr.

Jim, to work as an assistant cook on a cattle drive to Colorado. He proves himself a good scout with an uncanny ability to "read" the landscape, but Mr. Jim dies suddenly, leaving Thad on his own again. Through a series of coincidences, Thad is hired as a scout for an eminent paleontologist from Harvard, Professor George Babcock. Accompanying Babcock's expedition to the Judith River Badlands region of Montana, Thad travels with General Custer through the Black Hills and establishes close relationships with a band of Sioux, the young Black Elk in particular.

The fierce competition for fossils among the leading paleontologists of the day fuels the remaining plot. The setting shifts to England, where Dr. Algernon DeMott, a noted English paleontologist, is also preparing for a fossil-hunting expedition to Montana with his son Julian. When they arrive in New York, Julian meets a man involved with the New World Museum, a young institution that plans to reassemble and display the fossilized remains of dinosaurs that are being discovered. The idea of such a museum was radical at that time; most paleontologists were keeping their finds for their own collections or using them for study at elite universities.

Eventually, Julian and Thad meet in Montana, finding that despite the differences in their respective backgrounds, they have much in common. They especially share a dislike of the skullduggery used by the three competing teams of paleontologists who have converged on the area—a Professor Cunningham from Yale has also arrived—to sabotage each other's work. All three are more interested in inflating their own reputations than in furthering scientific knowledge.[8] When the two boys discover the fossilized remains of an enormous dinosaur, they join forces to excavate it in secret and decide to donate the bones to the New World Museum.

The fossil-hunting plot intersects with the historical conflict between the Great Plains Indians and government troops over control of lands belonging to Native Americans. Lasky uses actual events and characters in this subplot to dramatize the injustices inflicted upon Native Americans during the latter half of the nineteenth century and to expose Custer and other mythologized figures of history as blustering, unscrupulous fools. Again, she has sniffed out her rat.

Like the protagonists in *Journey* and *Divide,* Thad and Julian each undertake a figurative and literal journey to places that are new both geographically and psychologically. Although they begin from very different starting points, they arrive at similar destinations.

Thad, orphaned early and growing up without adult guidance in the gritty environment of a Texas saloon, wonders as he contemplates the night sky what he might become. Nothing in his early experiences hints at the answer. At the outset, he is not only "apart," independent and self-reliant of necessity, but completely alone. He articulates his situation succinctly when he meets the Sioux Black Elk: "I have no people."[9]

His misfortunes, however, have fortified him. He knows that whatever lies ahead, it cannot "be worse than that from which he had come" (*BW,* 9). Although he feels that the dual loss of his mother and Mr. Jim has made him "creakier with the weight of memory" (24), he develops a sure instinct for survival. And he acquires a passion for fossil hunting. Earlier, his ambition was to scout for some wealthy and powerful men on a hunting expedition. Now, his work as part of Professor Babcock's team has fostered a reverence for life, and he replaces his dream of "bringing living animals to death" with the "real thrill ... of bringing extinct animals nearer to life" (115).

Accompanying this change is a shift in his attitude toward Native Americans, which parallels Meribah's in *Divide.* Initially, he looks upon all Indians as potentially dangerous enemies, imagining that as a scout he can help hunters avoid Cheyenne and Sioux. Later, when he drinks water from Black Elk's injured and bloody hand, he becomes a blood brother to the young Sioux.

Black Elk's spirit can travel long distances, and Thad, who is deeply intuitive (like many of Lasky's protagonists), communes with him as he continues his journey toward Montana. When he climbs a peak in the Black Hills with Babcock and his team, he senses that Black Elk has climbed that same peak, and Thad can see the vista through his eyes, an echo of Meribah's wordless bond with the Iroquois Mrs. Grant. At that moment he feels "trapped between two visions—the ageless vision of an ancient people and that of his companions, hard, bright, and new" (*BW,* 114). With the vision comes an insight: the white man is wrong to claim the Black Hills, grounds sacred to the Sioux. He begins to see the westward expansion as a violation, the work of the greedy fossil hunters as a profanity. Subsequently, during the battle of Little Powder between Indian warriors and government soldiers, he rescues a Sioux baby from a burning tipi. The grateful Sioux bestow upon him a warrior's feather and a Sioux name: Man-Who-Runs-Through-Fire. He is no longer alone.

Thad has grown up illiterate, but the compassionate wife of Buffalo Bill Cody gives him an initial lesson in literacy, and slowly he teaches himself to read and write. He also gains a thorough education in paleontology and geological history. By the time he severs his ties with Professor Babcock, Thad has developed a deep respect for the land and the buried treasure of a past world that it holds. In a letter to Babcock explaining why he is leaving the expedition, he writes that "one of the troubles with learning is that you start getting ideas of your own" (*BW,* 323).

The novel's epilogue, set 56 years later, illustrates where those ideas have taken Thad. He has gained a notable reputation as a paleontologist, owns a 10,000-acre cattle ranch, and is the patriarch of a large family that includes a devoted wife descended from the Boston Cabots and several children and grandchildren. He now has "people." He is writing his own story, and the last sentence of the book circles back to its beginning, repeating the sentence that introduces his mother's murder: "His ma must not have known that the buffalo hunter was coming" (*BW,* 370). Like a Horatio Alger hero, he has journeyed from rags to respectability, richly rewarded for his integrity, native intelligence, and willingness to work hard.

In contrast, Julian begins his journey as the privileged son of an aristocratic scientist and is tutored in Latin, art, and the classics. Like Thad, however, he is motherless. His mother died giving birth to him, and the members of his household refer to the year of his birth only as the date of his mother's death. Julian accepts the omission stoically; he reflects that, given his father's profession, extinction seems to be the "business" of the house. Still, the absence of the mother he never knew resonates within him, and he imagines "how much fun it would be to sit at a table with other children" (BW, 22). He is very much alone, although hardly "apart," subjected as he is to his father's absolute control.

From Dr. DeMott's first appearance in the story, it is clear that despite his learning, his competence as both scientist and father is doubtful. Although he knows that paleontological discoveries have increasingly supported evolutionary theory, DeMott refuses even to consider such a notion, refuting as preposterous the idea that humans evolved from other forms of life. Instead, he is convinced of a "Divine Plan" that created man as its most complex and glorious culmination. Julian initially admires his father's theories, but like Thad he eventually formulates his own (more enlightened) views. Furthermore, DeMott is an egotist and a bully. His verbal abuse of Julian's art tutor demonstrates the "almost volcanic" anger that floods Julian with a terrible fear and foreshadows the moral depths to which DeMott later sinks.

Once in America, Julian is impressed by the vastness of the West. En route to Montana, while gazing upon the Nebraska prairie from a train window, he suddenly knows that although he has never protested his father's domination, "in this land the grip would loosen.... Life would change for him in a landscape of such scale and dimension," and he feels the "first stirrings within himself of his own power" (BW, 69).

During the expedition in Montana, DeMott reveals an even darker side of his character. He lies readily to deceive the competing teams of paleontologists and hires a scoundrel named Bobber Henshaw as a spy. The two men appear linked by a bond that "insulated them against any kind of reason or moral judgment" (BW, 225). Later, as Julian witnesses his father and Henshaw counterfeiting religious symbols of the Sioux to mislead the other teams, he is struck by a cruel irony: his father's hand forging the sacred markings has "written volumes on theories of God and law and the history of the earth" (151). The irony is compounded because DeMott is a bigot who has mocked the significance of the signs he now counterfeits. His pronouncement that all Indians are "destined to recede and perish due to their inferiority" runs counter to Julian's growing empathy with them (248–49). Julian sees his first Indians from his train window as General Sheridan, a fellow passenger, pontificates upon the "savages" and announces the government's intention to round up all Indians on reservations within the next two years.

As Julian studies the "vacant-eyed" Indian women squatting by the station door and contrasts their subservient demeanor with that of his arrogant fellow travelers, the "grand scale that had impressed him so much before suddenly contracted. The world seemed to shrink" (*BW*, 71). Although unschooled in the brief history of the United States, Julian intuitively judges this new country by how it treats some of its most vulnerable and least fortunate members. The issue of ownership—of Indian lands and the fossils they yield—moves Julian further from his father. He finds himself questioning his father's conviction that private collections are the proper destination of the bones being unearthed, and as competition among the three teams of paleontologists grows nastier, Julian knows that eventually he will "have to decide where he [stands]" (189).

As if to hasten Julian's growing alienation, DeMott brazenly takes credit for fossils that another member of his team has discovered. When Julian protests his father's claim, DeMott authorizes Bobber Henshaw to beat his son, instructing him to deliver "blows only to the backside," nothing that will "show" (*BW*, 222). Humiliated and angered by the beating, Julian confronts his father, threatening to expose DeMott's dishonesty if he ever sets Henshaw upon Julian again. His warning constitutes a genuine declaration of independence. That he makes it not in England but in the United States underscores the intensity of the rebellion that will eventually carry him to emotional and intellectual independence. But the rift comes at a considerable cost. Julian feels guilty about his deteriorating relationship with his father, as if he were partly responsible: "If [Julian] had been better, more morally perfect, could he have persuaded his father to change?" (329). It also puts Julian in mortal danger when Henshaw pushes him into a deep crevice. He escapes only with Thad's help, a rescue that marks their first meeting.

DeMott then plots to kill Thad but dies when his scheme misfires, killing Henshaw as well. Julian is dazed by the loss of his father (much as the child Thad was by his mother's death) and feels as if he were in "a strangely silent bubble" (*BW,* 338). But Julian recovers quickly, and he and Thad finally manage to load their giant fossil on a steamboat won for them in a poker game and to deliver it to the New World Museum, receiving (of course) considerable publicity and acclaim.

In the epilogue we learn that Julian has been appointed director of that very museum and has served with distinction. He has married an Indian woman and is planing to visit Thad, then attend a granddaughter's college graduation. Like Thad and his literary predecessors Sashie and Meribah, he is now "apart" in that he enjoys control of his own life, but he is far from alone.

The Bone Wars is, among other things, an adventure story, and its plot structure contributes to the suspense, alternating between Thad's and Julian's stories. The alternation of the early chapters juxtaposes Thad's hardscrabble life with Julian's privileged one and creates tension: how will the two strands of the story come together? After the separate plot lines converge at the boys' first meeting, the focus shifts back and forth between DeMott's and Babcock's separate camps. This movement serves to heighten the suspense, only slowly revealing DeMott's machinations, which first sweep Julian, then Thad, into the maelstrom.

The Bone Wars weaves several major themes into its adventure story, most of them common to Lasky's fiction. First, there is the issue of persecution, explored here much as it is in *Divide.* Many of the white characters in the story demonstrate bigotry against the Indians that is as offhand as it is cruel. Although they describe the Indians as "wild," "bloodthirsty," and "savage," those terms apply more accurately to their own actions. On a train trip west, several "gentlemen travelers" mindlessly shoot a herd of buffalo from their windows, leaving the fallen animals to rot along the tracks. Government troops level entire Indian villages, deliberately killing women and children, and when Babcock's team climbs a peak in the Black Hills, they shoot off carbines to celebrate their achievement. Bobber Henshaw equates Indians with "every groundhog, rattlesnake, and toad," yet no Indian in the story indulges in behavior as venomous as his own. Although there are scenes in which Indians attack whites, they are motivated by self-defense, not greed or the arrogance of power.

Closely linked to persecution of the Indians is the concept of Manifest Destiny, the imperious notion that it was the white man's God-given destiny to conquer the American West and "gain its treasures" (*BW*, 37). The concept absolved those believing in it of any legal or ethical barriers to seizing Indian lands, despite government treaties that protected them. Cody justifies the betrayal with insolent self-righteousness: "There's a higher law operating than treaty law. White man's coming, no matter what. It's our destiny to be here" (289).

Julian learns that wealthy entrepreneurs, exercising their sense of entitlement to the land, are investing their dreams and millions of dollars in hopes of exploiting the West. But he questions that entitlement when he begins to understand that "this west, said to be our destiny, has a past ... so profound that it could make our brashest dreamers tremble" (*BW*, 39). Thad has similar regard for the fossils being unearthed: "Now he had come to think of time in the same way Crazy Horse thought of the earth. He had never thought of himself as owning the fossils he had taken out of the earth" (213).

The issue of the past and its relationship to the present grows inevitably out of this story of paleontological digs, developing it somewhat differently than *The Night Journey* does, with more emphasis on the need to respect it. For Thad, his digging for fossils teaches him to love the "peeling back of present time, leaving only the past with its layers of history" (*BW*, 194). As he learns about the Cretaceous sea and the swamp that once covered the Badlands, he gains a new perspective on human existence and feels deeply the brevity and insignificance of the human life span when it is measured against geological time. The three teams of paleontologists, on the other hand, in their haste and zeal to outdo each other, recklessly destroy the very land and fossils that they have been trained to preserve. Black Elk's prophecy that "bullets will rain from the sky and the gold will be ripped out of the earth and the people and the earth will die" serves as a mournful indictment of the ruin to come (132). When Thad observes that on a clear, dry morning the horizon is a "pinky-gray smudge" like the color of his mother's lips, there is an unspoken parallel: both have been irrevocably violated.

In this novel, as in *Beyond the Divide,* language plays an important role in constructing each person's reality, justifying offensive behavior and concealing—or revealing—unpleasant truths. Thad, who once aspired to be a scout for "big game hunting," later perceives the "sport" as "butchering, pure and simple" (*BW,* 181). When Babcock suggests to Thad that he "discreetly observe" DeMott's camp, another team member challenges him: "Discreetly observe, Professor? How does that differ from spying?" (199). Custer, whose interest in the Black Hills lies mostly in its gold, claims that his mission is to make the Black Hills "safe," a term that obscures his intention to wrest the territory from its rightful Sioux inhabitants.

Lasky points to *The Bone Wars* as her favorite among her young adult novels. It embraces, she says, "all the things I love": history, paleontology, the American West. Indeed, there is much to admire here. Lasky's ambitious story embraces a kaleidoscopic chapter in American history, and she has captured its intrigue. Pratt Library's Young Adult Advisory Board included the novel on its "Youth-to-Youth Books: A List for Imagination and Survival," and Yvonne A. Frey, writing for *School Library Journal,* said, "Lasky's characters are memorable.... This is poetically written historical fiction that will give young adult readers a real sense of a complex period of our history."[10] But reviewers also took issue with the scope of the novel (it runs to nearly four hundred pages), criticizing the chaotic plot that often staggers under its own weight. Susan Terris in a review for the *New York Times Book Review,* while praising Lasky for the thoroughness of her research, criticizes her for "trying to describe too much" and adds that "she has allowed herself to get mired in factual data."[11] *Publishers Weekly* agreed: "While there are plenty of adventures, fascinating cameos, and intriguing suggestions about the ethics of the characters, the story never finds its central course."[12]

One can hardly argue differently, for the pacing of *The Bone Wars* is uneven. So many characters come and go that the narrative spins out of control, leaving the reader to wonder what to make of all these hotel managers, tutors, student paleontologists, hunters, Sioux warriors, and gamblers. What does Calamity Jane contribute to the story other than some local color, of which there is already a surfeit? Where does the incident with Wu Chow, the Chinese cook, and his aphrodisiac of ground dinosaur bones take us? The reader is served up ample chunks of information about an amazing range of subjects whose relevance is not always clear: in addition to many facts about Indian customs, prehistoric biology, geological history, and methods of excavating and preserving fossils, there are details about life in Boston's upper social strata, the ways of southern belles, the design of a nineteenth-century camp kitchen, and the life of riverboat gamblers. As Terris notes, the "admirable balance between historical detail and plot" that Lasky achieved in *The Night Journey* and *Beyond the Divide* is missing here.

Also, some unpleasant (although historically accurate) details burden the story. A drunk vomits on Thad's buckskins, and prostitutes hover in the background. Zena Sutherland wondered in the *Bulletin of the Center for Children's Books* why "the book begins with a scene in which five-year-old Thad is under a bed in which his mother, a prostitute, is being murdered by a brutal customer."[13] A good question. Lasky has answered it by saying that this incident is a "critical element in the development of Thaddeus' character. By the end of the novel, we know the formidable odds that he overcame and have a better appreciation of his character" ("Kitty," 163). Perhaps. If the scene were more integral to Thad's development, Lasky's argument would be more convincing, the prologue less problematic. As it is, Thad's characterization hardly hinges on his surmounting the trauma of his mother's murder. After the first chapter, he never reflects on it and reflects only rarely on his mother; it is his orphaned state, not the cause of it, that shapes his character and engages our interest as readers. His development rests mostly on his growing ties to the land and its fossils, his empathy for the Indians of the West, and his friendship with Julian.

We might question, too, the purpose of the other allusions to prostitution: Cody's wife refers scornfully to her husband's visiting "certain people who shall remain nameless" (*BW,* 59), a police sergeant who proves himself too "green" while at a brothel receives a rebate from a prostitute, and during a discussion about Wu Chow's love potion, one of the men comments that the "girls at the Hang It Up don't have much truck with Chinamen" (257). Lasky has defended the inclusion of these details with a historian's relish for the telling point: "A preponderance of the women who went West alone were or became prostitutes. Despite this fact, we prefer to think of them as school marms. Well, guess what? There weren't all that many schools out there, and, brace yourself, I discovered the existence of more than a few schoolmarms/prostitutes" ("Kitty," 164). Granted, but as with the opening scene, the problem is one of relevance. *The Bone Wars* is, after all, fiction, not history. It is Thad's and Julian's story, and just what the prostitutes at the Hang It Up contribute to it remains questionable.

Lasky's handling of dialogue, usually so sure, is uneven here. Julian's British dialect grows more pronounced at odd moments. Although his voice is hardly distinguishable from Thad's most of the time, near the end of the book his speech is marked by some intrusive British expressions, such as "bloke" and "old boy." Thad, who has hardly led a sheltered life, priggishly substitutes "darn" and "heck" for their profane equivalents. And sometimes the dialogue grows coy. When Thad and Julian design slat seats to make themselves more comfortable while hanging from rope slings to excavate fossils from a cliff, Julian exclaims, "If sore butts could sing hosannas, ours would!" (*BW,* 310). Also, the narrative viewpoint shifts unpredictably, so that the story, whose viewpoint is mostly limited to Thad's and Julian's, is briefly and unaccountably seen through the eyes of a Ree scout, Harvard student Jonathan Cabot, and—most inexplicably of all—General Custer. The shifts are especially disorienting in a novel already cluttered with an abundance of scenes, characters, and information.

After the plethora of people and places preceding it, the epilogue wraps things up too neatly. Like *The Night Journey,* this novel takes us into the future, but here it resolves questions the novel has hardly raised: Whom did Thad and Julian marry? What professions did they enter? Where did they live? And so on. Nonetheless, *The Bone Wars* offers to readers willing to mine its gold a cast of memorable characters, an education in paleontology, and a vivid slice of American western history.

Lasky's historical novel for middle-school readers *Alice Rose and Sam* is also set in the American West of the last century. However, her interest in nineteenth-century American history is hardly limited to the old West. A longtime resident of Cambridge, Massachusetts, Lasky has a lively interest in Boston and its environs, and she has often used it as a setting for both her children's and her adult fiction. In *True North,* Boston provides both a physical and a political locale for Lasky's suspenseful story of two young women who meet on the Underground Railroad on the brink of the Civil War years.

True North

Lasky remembers little of the antebellum American history she was taught as a schoolgirl in Indianapolis during the 1950s; slavery was presented as "wrong," but the more savage details were omitted. She learned almost nothing, for example, about how slave families were torn apart or how black girls and women were sexually exploited. And her quaint notion of the Underground Railroad was something akin to a Disneyland ride. In other words, she knew "some of the facts, but not the deeper truth."[14]

Then, through her own children's history curriculum in the Cambridge public schools, she discovered just how much she had missed. Smelling her rat, she began to study the history of slavery in the United States. The first-person accounts given by fugitive slaves especially intrigued her. The next step was predictable: "I decided I wanted to write a book about the Underground Railroad, about the men and women who rode on it and those station masters and agents who made it work." The result is *True North,* published in 1996.

True North bears certain similarities to Lasky's earlier historical fiction, particularly in its handling of narrative viewpoint and structure. Like *The Bone Wars,* this novel juxtaposes the alternating perspectives of two very different characters: Afrika, a young runaway slave known to her owner as Frieda; and Lucy Bradford, the youngest member of one of Boston's most distinguished families.[15] Like *Beyond the Divide, True North* opens very late in its plot, circles back to recount earlier events, then closes with an epilogue that summarizes Lucy's and Afrika's adult years.

An entry from Lucy's diary dated 1917 introduces the story. The elderly Lucy remembers a day 59 years earlier in Boston when, hidden from view, she secretly watched her sister's marriage ceremony. Her family, who believed that Lucy had drowned months earlier, were stunned and incredulous when they discovered her, very much alive, during the wedding reception. Only in the closing chapters of the book does the reader learn that Lucy feigned her own death to help Afrika escape.

The story then travels back to 1858 and south to Virginia, where Harriet Tubman is leading a group of escaped slaves northward. Afrika, however, hangs back. She has given premature birth to a daughter conceived when she was raped by her plantation overseer, and she insists on remaining with the frail child until it dies. Miss Harriet reluctantly moves on, and Afrika now must make her way alone, following the North Star to Canada and freedom. The alternations between Afrika's oppressed life and Lucy's privileged one underscore the contrast between the two and provide abundant historical information about both.

Through Lucy's strand of the story, set in and around Boston, the reader learns fascinating details about Bostonian social customs among the upper class—women, for example, were expected to keep their new gowns wrapped in tissue for a year to show proper restraint—and more important, about the ambiguous political temper of the times in Boston regarding the slavery issue. Many of Boston's leading families, contrary to popular perception, supported the South. The northern mills depended for their cotton on a slave-based economy, and as Lucy's father observes, "[L]iberal sympathies are going right out the window as they contemplate the future of their mills without a good steady flow of cotton" (*TN,* 66). Lasky puts the case even more directly in an author's note appended to the novel: "I came to realize that slavery could not have made it out of the seventeenth century . . . if it had not been for the support of such cities in the North like Boston" (261). To dramatize the impact of Massachusetts' Fugitive Slave Act, Lasky develops intriguing characters, both historic and fictitious, whose response to the law defines them. Some, like Lucy's grandfather Levi Bradford,[16] or Pap as she calls him, are abolitionists involved in the Underground Railroad; others are informants and false agents whose sympathies—and economic interests—lie with the South.

Afrika's story is told through page-turning episodes of her flight north. These are interspersed with flashbacks about her days as a slave on the plantation. Her escape is harrowing, a journey that recalls Meribah's story in its hardships and desperate fight for survival. Afrika's flight says much about the indomitable will to freedom and the perils that escaped slaves were willing to risk for it. Afrika must avoid capture by dogs, slave catchers, and spies. She must forge a river, slog through swamps, wade through a Boston sewer. She hides in a barrel beneath layers of oysters, in a coffin beneath a corpse. But she never thinks of giving up.

Her flashbacks, set in italics and often framed in dream sequences, paint a horrifying picture of slavery: black children wrested from their parents and sold, black girls and women raped by their overseers and masters, slaves whose fingers and toes have been amputated because they were caught praying or learning to read. Lasky renders the details of these and other practices—the brutal whippings, the auctions—in direct and searing language.

Afrika's trip on the Underground Railroad ends when she finds a hiding place inside a clock in Pap's study. However, Pap has died, and it is Lucy who discovers the fugitive. After narrowly eluding a determined slave catcher, the two young women make their way to the Canadian border, where they part company. The epilogue, dated 1919, brings the story full circle with a reunion in Pap's house between the two women, now in their seventies.

Although *True North* is rich in the kind of vivid detail that informs Lasky's other historical fiction, it has been stripped of the encyclopedic digressions of its predecessors. Lasky's editor insisted that the novel remain taut. "We put *True North* on a lean diet," Lasky says. "I learned a lot from writing it." The result is a plot whose pace is considerably faster than her earlier historical novels. The chapters are short, most less than 10 pages, and often close with a cliff-hanger. Chapter headings indicate dates and places, a device that helps readers chart the swift current of events. The shifts between Lucy's and Afrika's chapters are abrupt, with no attempt to make the kind of smooth transitions Lasky used in *The Night Journey*. The disjunction underscores the contrast between their two lives.

Readers familiar with Lasky's earlier historical fiction will recognize the same concern for the oppressed (obviously, in this case, the enslaved and fugitive blacks) and the same outrage at the oppressors' cruelty. Here, too, is the view of language as a powerful determinant of each person's reality. Mr. de Rosey, for instance, a southerner who is actually an unscrupulous slave catcher, passes himself off as a refined businessman up north "representing Southern interests" (*TN*, 187). And Lucy's affectionate nickname for her grandfather, Pap, is to her older sister's ears only an offensive "pickaninnish" moniker slave children use for old men. Lucy says, "[P]eople have a convenient way of molding realities to fit their own illusions" (256). Lasky demonstrates that language provides the means for doing so.

Readers will also recognize Lasky's skillful characterizations. Vivid physical descriptions and lively, often humorous dialogue give even the minor characters life and dimension. The characters speak a range of dialects, from proper Bostonian to slave vernacular to that of a Maine sailor. Lasky handles all successfully. The dialect never obscures meaning or carries any hint of condescension. As in *The Night Journey,* elderly characters are treated with sensitivity and empathy. Pap in particular is engaging and complex: he is gentle but also tough, shrewd as well as learned. Like Nana Sashie, he has forged a strong bond with the youngest member of his family, providing the "northing" of her moral compass that Lucy's sisters lack. The novel is also marked by Lasky's unerring sense of place. Both the Virginia swamp and the streets of Boston are vividly presented, the setting as integral to the story as are its characters. Her imagery, too, effectively conveys the emotional impact of events. When Pap dies, his hand slipping from Lucy's, he is "gone, swift as a sloop over the horizon with a following breeze" (*TN*, 182).

Lucy and Afrika are in many ways typical of Lasky's young adult protagonists: determined, courageous, intelligent, principled. They are both intuitive, able (like Thad and Black Elk) to comprehend each other's thoughts without words, and they are smart, quick to make sense of what on the surface appears incomprehensible. Both study the heavens, Lucy learning to use the constellations to chart a sailing course and Afrika searching the heavens for the North Star. In Lasky's fiction, characters with their eyes on the heavens invariably deserve a place there. Her villains are more concerned with earthbound affairs.

Like Lasky's other female protagonists, Lucy chafes at the constraints imposed by gender. She finds especially tedious the task of embroidering monograms on her sister's wedding linens, a "cruel custom that yoked every female relative and every female servant in the bridal household to an embroidery hoop" (*TN*, 9–10). And she enjoys sailing with Pap because on board "it didn't seem to matter that she had been born a girl" (61). The epilogue makes clear that Lucy's marriage has not dampened her unorthodox thinking: she has insisted on keeping an independent bank account and setting up a trust for special causes, which she manages herself. Her husband, now deceased, surely was unusual for his time: he "supported his wife in all her endeavors" (254).

Lucy's resistance to social mores is reminiscent of Jo March in Louisa May Alcott's *Little Women;* she, like Jo, is impatient with the protocols that dictate female dress and behavior and is often therefore at odds with her highly conventional family. Even Lucy's name singles her out as being different; her sisters (Iris, Rose, Delphinia, and Daisy) are named after flowers, but Lucy's name aligns her with Bradford family ships whose appellations all include the word *light*. Pap explains that "Lucy" is derived from the word *lux*, Latin for light, and he declares this a particularly apt choice because of Lucy's delicate touch on the wheel of his sailing ship. Lucy is also a guiding light, Afrika's earthly equivalent of the North Star. During one of her dreams, the fugitive realizes the parallel: "A star come down from heaven to lead me" (*TN*, 220).

Lucy likes her name but not the feeling of being so different from the rest of her family. She feels very much alone, except when she is with Pap. It "would be much nicer, less strange," she thinks, "to fit in" (*TN*, 78–79). Her mother finds her outspoken daughter "freakish," and like Meribah, Lucy squirms at feeling so "peculiar." She guesses that her mother loves her, but "neither one understood the other" (68). Lucy's emotional distance from her family, her sense of being "alone" while in their company, contrasts with Afrika's yearning for family, for the mother she lost as an infant. It also links Lucy to her counterparts in Lasky's contemporary novels, all of whom ponder the question of what it means to belong to a "family."

Lucy finds her family life boring, dominated as it is by plans for her sister's wedding. She even hopes for a hurricane with winds strong enough to "blister the varnish off wood" and welcomes the excitement promised by an owling expedition with Pap (*TN*, 8). In the silent, dark woods her sense of being alone finds a correlative in the mysterious blackness, but even as it frightens her she recognizes its beauty. She hopes someday to find in the woods "a calm, in the night a refuge, and even an unspoken meaning" (113).

Given Lucy's longing for excitement and her resistance to what she sees as pointless social customs, it is no surprise that her sympathies are readily enlisted to the cause of fugitive slaves. Through Pap, she learns that it is better to break an immoral law than to abide by it, and she shares his scorn for a court "obliged to sit protected by bayonets" (*TN*, 135). Like Sarah of *Pageant*, her soul harbors a guerrilla, and she is undeterred by her youth and physical vulnerability. Rather, she remembers the great horned owl she has observed in the woods, fragile but lethal as it moved in for a successful kill. "One did not have to be all muscle and brawn to vanquish," she reflects (123). It is a lesson she takes to heart when she and Afrika are nearly caught by Mr. de Rosey as they flee from Boston.

The action of *True North* is less inward than in some of Lasky's earlier fiction. In this novel, the emphasis is more on the escalating suspense than on the individual development of Lucy and Afrika. As the network of spies and slave catchers close in on them and their adventures culminate in Afrika's escape into Canada, the two girls remain passionate, clear sighted, and independent—but little changed. There is one exception: Lucy realizes a newfound strength. Surviving illness in the chilly fall weather while accompanying Afrika to the Canadian border, she finds in the still, dark night the unspoken meaning she has sought. She will never be lonely again.

Reviewers gave *True North* unanimous accolades. Almost all applauded the strong characterizations of Lucy and Afrika and the vivid rendering of this particular chapter of American history. "A rousing good story," said *Kirkus Reviews*.[17] "An excellent work of history, carefully researched and poignantly told," echoed *School Library Journal*.[18] *Booklist* praised Lasky's "rich imagery and detail," "suspenseful plot," and "vivid and believable" characters, calling the novel "stimulating, soul-stirring historical fiction."[19] *Publishers Weekly* gave the work a starred review and noted that "Lasky again combines suspenseful fiction with history" and told her story "with sensitivity and flair."[20] *True North* is in many ways Lasky's most accomplished historical fiction, a novel that aptly balances scholarly, insightful research with an engrossing, memorable story.

Conclusion

Taken together, *Beyond the Divide*, *The Bone Wars*, and *True North* represent a range of historical fiction for young adults, novels that conform to some conventions of the genre and departs from others. Like all good historic or historical fiction, these novels convey an immediate sense of time and place. The period and setting of each is integral to its story, serving as much more than a quaint backdrop and anchoring the narrative in very particular ways. Each novel also demonstrates the flow of history from the past into the present, allowing us, as Donelson and Nilsen say, "to realize that despair is as old, and new, as hope, that loyalty and treachery, love and hatred, compassion and cruelty, were and are inherent in humanity." (Donelson and Nilsen, 169).

All three, too, follow the pattern of what Donelson and Nilsen call "adventure/accomplishment romances," an archetypal quest structure in which the protagonist is separated from a nurturing community of friends and family, undergoes an ordeal or crisis that tests his or her courage and stamina, and having passed the test successfully, is "reunited with former friends and family in a new role of increased status" (Donelson and Nilsen, 125–27). Lasky varies the pattern somewhat in these three novels. As we have seen, she takes her young protagonists through the stages of separation and testing, as the archetype requires, but only Lucy is "reunited" with people from her earlier life. Each of the others creates a new life under dramatically altered circumstances, severing connections with their former worlds and forging new bonds in new places for their emerging adult selves.

As might be expected, none of the young protagonists in these novels is plagued with the self-absorption and angst that afflict adolescents in much young adult fiction. All have more critical matters at hand as they face challenges to their very survival. Their journeys bring them face to face with profound moral issues of their day, and as they position themselves in relation to these ethical questions, they search for spiritual direction, uncertain of their place as "particles" in the vast universe. Whether tracing the journey of the stars across the night sky or observing the dance of a dust mote, they ponder the existence of a higher power, wanting to be part of a larger pattern or order. Thus, when they do stop to consider the meaning of life or their own individual lives, it is—to a degree unusual in young adult fiction—more a groping toward a cosmic view than an inward examination of self, a refreshing perspective for YA literature.

Adolescence, then, in the three novels discussed in this chapter, is a serious matter, constrained by an unspoken but consistent code of ethics. The young protagonists of these stories seem oblivious to matters that absorb many of their fictional counterparts—appearance, emerging sexuality, popularity with peers. Although they rebel against injustices perpetuated by their elders, they accord automatic courtesy to most adults. They are unfailingly loyal to those who merit their allegiance, are deeply idealistic, and have the courage of their convictions. All but Lucy are cultural outsiders, ultimately triumphant over what, realistically, are nearly insurmountable obstacles. It is an engaging and inspiring picture that Lasky has drawn in these three novels, and their protagonists provide both a comparison and a contrast to their counterparts in Lasky's contemporary novels for young adults.

5. Contemporary Lives: Family and Friends

"What is a family?" asks 16-year-old Birdie Flynn, the protagonist of *Prank,* the first of Lasky's novels set entirely in the present. Published in 1984, it probes Birdie's question in considerable depth, exploring a theme that also shapes Lasky's next two novels with contemporary settings, *Home Free* and *Pageant.* Lasky always involves her characters in issues that transcend their individual problems, but the protagonists of these three novels are ultimately concerned with matters of family, with defining its nature and discovering their place in one.

Prank

Birdie's family is, as she puts it, thoroughly "messed-up," and *Prank* opens with an ugly crisis in the Flynn household. Birdie's 17-year-old brother, Timmy, a habitual troublemaker at school, has just been charged, along with two of his friends, with defacing a synagogue. This act of vandalism—or "prank," as Birdie's family defensively and inappropriately labels it—serves as a catalyst, affecting the Flynns in ways that none of them can foresee at the outset. Eventually, the change is for the better, but it is slow and painful in coming.

In some ways, this story is about the role that change plays in our growth as human beings and the harmful effects of human inflexibility. It is also about the willingness to acknowledge responsibility for one's behavior as a necessary prelude to changing it. Birdie's family is locked into responses that are ineffectual at best, physically and emotionally damaging at worst. Quick to argue, they spout offensive generalizations about Jews (who are "taking over"), "wops" ("smart" and "fabulous gardeners"), and businesswomen (all "lesbians"). Birdie's father, Joe, reacts to frustration by lashing out with his tongue or his fists, attacking his children with words or blows or both. Her mother, Marge, harps on her children's limitations, on what they should not attempt and cannot accomplish. A devout Catholic, she often escapes in prayer to the Virgin Mary. Both parents are blind to what they are doing to their children. Birdie's older sister, Lainie, has replicated the destructive family pattern by marrying an abusive husband, and she regularly runs back home with her four-year-old daughter, Rhonda. A television set drones on in the living room, counterpointing the family's incessant bickering with the sound track from the vapid children's programs that Rhonda watches constantly.

Birdie herself longs for change, but in the aftermath of the "prank," she fears that nothing will alter her family. "Maybe the Flynns weren't smart enough to change," she thinks, even as her own priorities are shifting.[1] When we first meet Birdie, her dreams are focused on escaping from her quarrelsome family and her shabby, working-class neighborhood in east Boston. She wants desperately to be "apart" from her parents, to share a nice apartment across the harbor with her best friend, Gloria. To that end, she and Gloria have taken summer jobs in the basement of Filene's department store, and Birdie eagerly anticipates the designer jeans she will buy with her employee discount.

In the early chapters, Birdie is frequently preoccupied by thoughts of clothes. Her pursuit of fashion would be comical were it not so pathetic. She emulates the look of a popular model by plucking her eyebrows into tortured arches and browses among the merchandise displayed at Filene's to note what is "in," so eager to follow the latest styles that she purchases a linen blazer identical to Gloria's. From her perch on a pier in the Boston harbor, Birdie looks west to the upscale neighborhood across the harbor and thinks, "That's where the jeans [are] . . . and the designer shoes and bags and all the stuff that [has] signatures and initials, those stamps of style and taste and belonging" (*Prank*, 26). Timmy is on the mark when he derides Birdie's desires as "franchise dreams."

Her yearning for trendy clothes is matched by an equally strong fixation on being thin. She longs to be as "skinny" as Gloria, who wears size four jeans. To ward off unwanted pounds, Birdie abstains from pizza, eats "sandwiches" without bread and salad without dressing. She seeks refuge in the school library because it is a "place for thinking and dreaming and not worrying about getting fat" (*Prank*, 5). Only gradually do these concerns yield to more consequential ones as she becomes less focused on herself. She teaches Lainie how to keep account books for her new venture selling cosmetics door-to-door, thus helping to liberate her sister from an unhappy marriage, and she encourages Timmy to apply for a job on a tugboat, a move that changes his life. Most significant, she begins to read about the Holocaust and makes connections between its almost unimaginable evil and Timmy's "prank."

Lasky often touches on the theme of bigotry in her young adult fiction, graphically portraying the dehumanizing effect of unchecked hatred upon the perpetrators as well as on the victims. In this novel, the theme manifests itself through the prank and what Birdie learns about the Holocaust by reading Elie Wiesel's *Night* and the autobiography of Rudolph Hoess, commandant of Auschwitz. She responds similarly to both: she is shamed by Timmy's "prank," as if the whole family were "caught" in it, and feels somehow implicated in the Holocaust, a reaction that magnifies the horror of what she reads. She is appalled when she realizes that Hoess exonerated himself from wrongdoing in the same language that Timmy used to excuse his participation in the prank: each of them only watched—"had to watch," they said, as if they had no choice and as if only watching absolved them of responsibility.

Lasky raises the nagging questions of guilt and responsibility in unflinching terms, making clear that each person, under even the most extreme circumstances, is accountable for his own choices. Birdie tries to imagine the lives of the Nazi officers who ran the death camps. Did they send cards home to their families for Christmas and birthdays? What were their thoughts as they saw smoke from the gas ovens darken the skies? She is stunned to discover that evil is not always easily identified, not always "bloody. It's gray, too, and dingy and boring and ordinary" (*Prank,* 91), a perception that echoes Hannah Arendt's ironic observations about "the banality of evil."[2]

It seems impossible to Birdie that during the war her parents were planting gardens and playing on the beach while, across the ocean, whole families were incinerated. How could two such different worlds have existed simultaneously? How, in the aftermath of such horror, can the sun continue to shine? Things become "strangely discontinuous" for Birdie. This sense of discontinuity is reflected in the novel's structure. There are 23 short chapters that shift time, place, and tone without transitions: a somber note that closes one chapter is often followed by a chirpy sentence opening the next. For example, after Birdie observes in her diary that her family seems "like six random people sitting in a room together" where the silence is deafening, the next chapter begins with Gloria asking, "Want to cruise designer sportswear?" (130–31).

The novel is written in the third person and limited mostly to Birdie's point of view. However, her diary entries allow a shift to the first person and the language of an adolescent girl. Lasky often uses the strategies of mimetic fiction—letters and essays as well as diaries written in the voice of a main character—to convey a convincing immediacy. In this instance, the diary allows Lasky to explore one of her most forceful and recurrent themes: the intrusion of the past upon the present. Although Birdie's father dismisses the death camps as "history" that he can't "undo," Birdie's anguish as expressed in her diary demonstrates that history is very much part of the present.

So strongly does the past affect Birdie that she finds herself fumbling for words when she tries to write about the camps, although she is an excellent English student whose papers earn praise from her English teacher and whose diary demonstrates a grasp of language that exceeds her years and education. But in writing about the Holocaust, she knows that "language would only trivialize it" (*Prank,* 90). Clearly, this is Lasky's point as well as Birdie's; the inadequacies of language to express our profoundest experiences is another theme that resonates in her novels.

Birdie's powerful reaction to what she learns about the Holocaust deepens her sense that a common humanity binds all people, a perception similar to Meribah's in *Beyond the Divide.* This feeling intensifies when, one evening, she sees her brother in a line of boys waiting to have sex with Phyllis "Fill 'er up" Dougherty. Birdie becomes physically ill, imagining herself instead of Phyllis at the end of that line. Later, paraphrasing John Donne's famous poem, she writes in her diary, "Any woman's submission diminishes me, because I am involved in womankinde" (*Prank,* 55). She knows in a direct and visceral way that no man—or woman—is an island.

Yet as she observes her uncommunicative family sitting in the living room, her father absorbed in the newspaper, her sister Lainie staring out the window, and her mother playing solitaire, she reflects that they are all islands or, as she phrases it, all solitaire players. Eventually she confronts her parents, challenging them to change, to believe in their children instead of programming them for failure. It is painful for her parents to face the corrosive role that they have played in their children's lives, but gradually the family tries to communicate without bickering. Birdie notes the progress in her diary: "It wasn't as if they were just trying to listen to each other. It was as if they were trying to hear for the first time ever" (*Prank,* 165).

By the novel's close, Birdie is enrolled in an internship program at the *Boston Globe* for high school seniors and has published an essay there that is ostensibly about Timmy but that speaks to the power of parental expectations and individual responsibility. As Birdie moves from being absorbed with her own weight to matters of true weight—the German death camps—she becomes a highly sympathetic character, compassionate and spirited. Although she is still in east Boston at the novel's close, she has, like Sashie and Meribah, made a long journey.

Prank is also Timmy's story, for Birdie's development is closely tied to his. At the outset, Timmy reads on a fourth-grade level and has earned three Fs and a D on his last report card. He seems a typical delinquent whose "antisocial behavior" has occasioned frequent visits to the principal's office; unable to look people in the eye while speaking with them, he has energy only for rage and destruction. But in his private conversations with Birdie, he demonstrates a quick intelligence, even wit. His fascination with the tugboats in the Boston harbor—the "dwarfs," as Birdie notes, that push the "giant" ships around—reflects his own sense of being a dwarf, a failure in nearly every way. As he explains to Birdie, he participated in the "prank" after a humiliating sexual episode in which he "wasn't able to do it" (*Prank,* 69). Like Birdie, he travels far. He moves out of his family's apartment to the tugboat and earns approval from his employers for his hard work there, perhaps his first experience with success. His rising self-esteem motivates him to improve his reading skills so he can study to become a certified navigator. He even apologizes in person for his act of vandalism, a substantial turning point for him.

The parallel stories of Birdie and Timmy provide an answer of sorts to Birdie's question "What is a family?" She herself never answers it directly, perhaps because the complexity of "family" defies tidy definition and because she finds herself caught in a paradox: although convinced that no person is an island, that she is part of the human family and "involved in womankinde," she nonetheless feels deeply the need to be "apart" from her own family, an impulse many of Lasky's adolescent protagonists share. They each discover that they must develop an autonomous self to negotiate the uneven road from childhood to adulthood (although the destructive atmosphere of the Flynn household invests Birdie's need with special urgency). "Family," then, becomes for Birdie a point of departure, for better or for worse, that marks the beginning of her journey toward a separate self and life.

Although there are instances in *Prank* that support the value of community—Joe Flynn remembers World War II as a "good time—everybody pulling together," and Birdie reflects that "maybe you could stand anything if you had someone to talk to" (*Prank,* 85, 155)—they are overshadowed by the novel's insistence on each person's need for being "apart." Timmy expresses the need succinctly in his reply to Birdie when she proposes that she, too, get a job on the tug: "You've got to let me have this for myself, for me, just me" (143).

The question of family raises the related issue of self, for it is within the family unit that a child's sense of self first emerges. What shapes it? What defines it? Like Meribah, Birdie has been defined by others, largely in terms of her gender. Her parents have assigned her a subordinate place in the family hierarchy not because of her age but because she is a female who should behave submissively. When Timmy is arrested, Marge appears more concerned with Birdie's single muttered swearword, her "unladylike talk," than with her son's being led away in handcuffs. If Birdie voices a contradictory opinion or challenges her parents in any way, they address her as "missy," a humiliating term intended to keep her at the bottom of the family pecking order. Birdie understands exactly how the word operates: "They call me missy to make me feel like a little girl—a powerless little girl," she writes in her diary (*Prank*, 40–41). And of course, much of Timmy's behavior can be traced to his parents' low expectations.

Popular culture, too, shapes one's sense of self, and this is particularly true for young people, whose identities are still in flux. Certainly Birdie's excessive concern about clothing and weight reflects a cultural obsession with a particular standard of female beauty. Similarly, the pressure that Timmy feels to perform sexually indicates a cultural view of male sexuality that Gloria articulates when she insists that all guys want to "do it" because that is "the way guys are" (*Prank*, 62).

Lasky's contemporary fiction often demonstrates sharp impatience with the follies of popular culture, and *Prank* provides an opportunity for some scathing commentary. She takes on not only fashion and sex but also the tricky promotional language of a materialistic culture. The descriptors in the names for Lainie's cosmetic merchandise—Exuberanza moisturizer, Red-As-All-Get-Out lipstick, and Desert Light blush—mock their real-life counterparts in their lack of any denotative meaning. Lainie's sales pitch is equally empty. She convinces her east Boston customers that the jet fumes from the nearby airport make their skin "age three times faster" (faster than what, she never specifies). When Birdie objects that this claim might be a lie, Lainie retorts that "it's usually a sale," especially when she uses words like "emissions, acidity and embedded particles" (*Prank*, 104). Even children as young as Rhonda are susceptible to the seductive language of advertising. She begs for the "Walk-Around Farm from Hasbro's Romper Room, each part sold separately, no assembly required" and wants to eat at a "participating McDonald's" (20). (Sardonic references to McDonald's crop up regularly in the dialogue of Lasky's contemporary characters, as we have already seen in *The Night Journey*. The golden arches seem to represent for Lasky all that is crass in modern culture.)

Religion, another shaping force, comes in for its share of criticism. Lasky's novels often reveal a rugged skepticism toward organized religion, and not surprisingly, Birdie finds no solace in the Roman Catholic faith of her parents. Her doubts about the church took root five years previously when the nuns preparing her for confirmation "short-circuited" her choice of Pinky as a name and made her substitute Rose instead. Now, she wonders cynically if the "Great Transformer" in the sky really cares about such matters. She mocks the chipped Madonna figure that her mother has stationed in the scrubby yard of the Flynn's apartment building by calling her "Our Lady of Perpetual Weeds" and views her mother's reliance on the Virgin as little more than an ineffectual sop (*Prank*, 107).

The more contact she has with the church, the more disillusioned she becomes. When Timmy takes a janitorial job at Our Lady of Victory church, where his immediate superior is a petty tyrant who lapses into baby talk when thwarted, Birdie thinks, "No victories to be racked up here" (*Prank*, 33). Her newfound knowledge about the Holocaust only sharpens her religious doubts. What kind of God could permit this to happen? she wonders, a question that haunts the book. To her parents' distress, she says that she no longer believes in God's existence.

The reader may not agree with her views but can surely understand what prompts them. The presence of evil in a world created by a supposedly benevolent deity is a much debated philosophical dilemma that has stumped minds wiser than Birdie's. In her novels Lasky often faults organized religion for its failure to deal with this question and to speak to our deepest needs. In *Prank* she uses the Roman Catholic Church to address this theme; in subsequent books she manifests equal irreverence toward other religions, but always to demonstrate the weakness of unexamined faith and autocratic dogma rather than to criticize any particular set of beliefs.

This novel received mixed notices. Lasky was praised for her characterization of the Flynns, especially Birdie. "[A]n engrossing portrait of female cultural emancipation," said one reviewer.[3] A "vivid character," said another who also faulted Lasky for creating a protagonist "too good, too able to effect change in her family."[4] Granted, Birdie's virtues are extraordinary. She is so bright that she can recall huge chunks of Hoess' autobiography and recite them verbatim to Timmy, so articulate that some of her dialogue and parts of her diary are almost implausibly eloquent, so erudite that her thoughts are sprinkled with casual literary allusions ranging from Homer to Hemingway, and so capable that she even edits a romance novel that Gloria's mother is attempting. However, fictional characters are always heightened, larger than life, and Lasky has taken pains to make credible Birdie's superior abilities and the Flynns' transformation, the latter of which comes about gradually and produces what is, even by the last chapter, hardly an ideal family.

More serious is the charge Albert Schwartz leveled in the *Interracial Books for Children Bulletin*. He writes, "After raising serious societal issues, the author ignores them, suggesting that anti-Semitism is due to troubled individuals rather than societal factors."[5] Indeed, presenting Timmy's "prank" as rooted in an unhappy home and his own sense of inadequacy rather than in any widespread social malice tends to minimize the very problem of bigotry that Lasky is addressing. Timmy is too readily sorry, too easily reformed to give full rein to a serious exploration of the issue. Nor, if his actions stem from the sins of his narrow-minded parents, can we logically account for Birdie, who comes out of the same environment.

Still, in both the seriousness of its major themes and the engaging quality of its main character, *Prank* offers a satisfying reading experience for young adults. Readers who know little about the Holocaust and the depth of its evil and who may have dismissed it as just "history" will surely gain a new perspective on those terrible years and on the contemporary significance of the past.

Home Free

Lasky's next young adult novel, *Home Free,* followed *Prank* by a year, in 1985. It too raises the question of family but articulates it in different terms. What, it asks, constitutes "home"? What does it mean to be "home"?

This is the story of Sam Brooks, who has just moved from Indiana, where he has lived all of his 16 years, to Massachusetts, his mother's native state. His father, killed more than a year ago, was the victim of a car crash with a drunken driver, and the widowed Phillipa Brooks is glad to be back in Massachusetts. Not so Sam. A large extended family—aunts, uncles, cousins, a grandparent—live nearby, but he feels desperately "alone." How, he wonders, can this new place be home for his mother but not for him? Will he find a home here?

For Sam, the answer lies in two unexpected friendships—one with Gus, a retired wildlife photographer dying of cancer, the other with Lucy, an autistic young girl who lives in the local Belchertown Home for the Homeless. Gus is fighting to live long enough to see a dream fulfilled: he hopes to save the "accidental wilderness" bordering the Quabbin Reservoir from developers who want to open the area for recreation. The reservoir was created 50 years earlier by flooding the Swift River Valley and four towns along its banks to provide a water supply for Boston; now Gus is trying to establish the area as a breeding ground for endangered eagles.

That the eagles are indeed endangered becomes clear early in the novel when Phillipa remembers a photograph her late husband took of an eaglet embryo. The eaglet had been born without a shell, "orphaned" before birth because the food supply of the parent eagle had been so heavily contaminated by chemicals. Thus Gus' project to introduce eagles into the "accidental wilderness" of the Quabbin, which is untouched by chemical sprays, acquires particular urgency and raises the larger issue of conservation.

However, resolving the competing priorities that vie to control the region—animal refuge versus human recreation—is no simple matter, and Lasky demonstrates, in a scene portraying a community meeting where the question is debated, just how compelling the arguments are on either side. She complicates the debate with characters whose family homes and lands were flooded when the reservoir was created and who consequently feel entitled to use the Quabbin for their own enjoyment.

There is no question, however, of where Lasky's sympathies lie. Here, as in *The Bone Wars,* she refutes the notion that humans are the highest form of life with an undisputed claim on the earth's resources. Sam notes that the 50-million-year history of birds "rather dwarfed in comparison the five or six million for people,"[6] and Gus ridicules the notion that the "sovereignty of the earth" belongs to "higher life forms, like . . . God-fearing Congregationalists" (*HF,* 153). In other words, the pleasures of humans do not automatically take precedence over the needs of animals, and opening the Quabbin to developers bodes ill for the latter. Sam's imagination takes a "doomsday turn" when he envisions the consequences of doing so, foreseeing "the golden arches of McDonald's looming up" in the area (167). Readers familiar with Lasky's view of the hamburger franchise know that this is doomsday indeed! However, with Sam's help, Gus' dream is realized, albeit after his death.

Lucy, too, realizes a dream through Sam's friendship. Lasky had read about autism and thought, "What is this world they inhabit?" To her, the condition seemed "a very good metaphor for someone who's cut off, disenfranchised." Lucy is indeed cut off, but with Sam's encouraging support she emerges from the prison of her autism and becomes involved with the eagle project along the way. Lucy's presence hints at a mysterious past and an uncanny connection with the eagles, especially with a majestic eagle named Ilirah, with whom Sam and Lucy learn to communicate. The mystery is resolved when the novel shifts into fantasy, and Sam, traveling back in time to witness Lucy's earlier life and death in one of the towns now flooded, learns that Ilirah has guarded Lucy's spirit during the intervening years, keeping it alive.

Sam shares much in common with Lasky's other young adult protagonists. He is knowledgeable about astronomy and conversant with a range of literature—works by Lewis Carroll, Thomas More, Marianne Moore, Clement Moore, Frank Baum, Robert and Elizabeth Browning, John Greenleaf Whittier, and John Masefield. Proficient with language, he occasionally writes poetry, adapting other writers' works to express his own ideas, just as Birdie has done. Like Lasky's female protagonists, he rebels against cultural gender stereotypes; he is aware that as a male adolescent he is expected to enjoy hunting and competitive sports, but he eschews both. Most significantly, he is "alone."

His loneliness at first accounts for his unusual relationships with Gus and Lucy. Drawn to them out of his need for companionship, Sam chides himself for making friends only with a dying "old codger" and a "nutso" girl. However, he is perhaps the most altruistic of Lasky's adolescent protagonists, and he grows to care deeply for both Gus and Lucy, offering friendship that is singularly generous. He willingly spends hours alone at night in the Quabbin wilderness, confined to a blind, to capture the eagles on film for Gus, who has been sidelined by his illness. The film, Gus has explained, will document the eagles' presence and help block plans to develop the Quabbin for recreation. Sam's long hours in the blind, where he learns to sit "without fear or longing or loneliness" (*HF*, 120), teach him the value of solitude, of being "apart," and help him overcome his grief over his father's death.

With Lucy, Sam senses that despite her blank and unresponsive manner, she is "oddly alert and attendant" to an inward reality (*HF*, 84). He, too, becomes alert to that strange world, finding his way into it much as he has maneuvered his way through the night wilderness of the Quabbin, willing to "leave off the day and the land and the known for a different order of things" (85). Lasky often creates highly intuitive characters, and that trait in Sam, coupled with his perceptiveness and magnanimity of spirit, serves well to lead Lucy into the real world.

  Sam's adjustment to his move east hinges on both of these friendships, for only through them is he able to create a new "family" and a new "home." Lasky plays with the meaning of home throughout the novel. The Belchertown Home where Lucy lives is, in fact, no home to her at all. The numerous skylights and floor-to-ceiling windows of the building's new wing create not a homey atmosphere but a "noiseless cross fire" of light so bright that the staff members wear sunglasses inside (*HF,* 76). The sunglasses seem emblematic of the staff's insensitivity to the residents' needs. One attendant calls Lucy "gal" instead of by her given name, intensifying the distance that Lucy's autism has already created, and a nurse in charge seems more concerned with Sam's welfare when he comes to visit than with that of Lucy herself. The doctors speak of Lucy in "hollow words" that represent her as a case, not a human being: they refer to her "autism," her "twiddling," her "toileting behavior." Sam is convinced that although his friendship with Lucy has been brief, he knows her better than all three of her doctors put together.

  Other references to "home" carry more positive connotations. In the first of two incidents that echo the book's title, Sam releases four eaglets that have been brought from Canada to the Quabbin, where they have been caged in a hacking tower for several weeks. If the project succeeds, the birds will imprint the area and return to nest and breed. However, there is no certainty that the eaglets, deprived of a parent bird's example, will know how to fly. The text implies a parallel to Sam, also orphaned and uprooted: "Without coach or guide . . . without the steady repetitive image of parent winging home—was it not an awesome proposition, the ultimate dare to grab the wind and break free alone?" (*HF,* 122). Only when the eaglets soar into the Quabbin wilderness do Sam and Lucy dare to hope that the project will attain its goal. As the last eaglet lifts into the air, Lucy turns to Sam, tears streaking her cheeks, and murmurs, "Home . . . free" (142).

Sam repeats that phrase when Lucy herself comes "home," not only physically to the site of Sam and Phillipa's house but spiritually to the "real" world of the present. In the penultimate chapter of the book, Lucy discovers that the eagle Ilirah has released her spirit because "it's time for me to come home." To which Sam replies, "Home free" (*HF*, 234). Both incidents seem to imply that one can be truly "home" only when one's spirit is unfettered and the home is home by choice.

"Home" acquires another layer of meaning when Sam and his mother finally take Lucy from the Belchertown Home to live with them. As they drive away from the institution, Phillipa says to her son, "Home, Sam?" " 'Yeah,' Sam replies. 'Home' " (*HF*, 241). His answer affirms that his place is now in Massachusetts with his newly constructed family, in the old house that his mother has worked to restore. On the final page of the novel, Ilirah too comes home, accompanied by a mate, her talons gripping a small branch for a nest in the Quabbin. Like his mother, Sam has also "restored" a home, this one for a family of eagles. Home, then, is that place—whether in the heart or in the external world—where one finds peace and purpose within one's family. And "family," as constructed in this novel, is less a matter of blood ties that one must loosen (as in *Prank*) than of nurturing relationships forged through mutual respect and affection.

Like *Prank*, *Home Free* ponders the inadequacies of language to express one's most heartfelt experiences. Sam, for example, is at first reluctant to talk about Lucy to his mother. Words, he feels, cannot describe her or represent his friendship with her, especially because his mother is a former English teacher, and words are her "thing." Words can also obstruct communication rather than facilitate it, as when a woman who advocates opening the Quabbin for more recreation maintains that the area is "underutilized." Phillipa challenges her statement, asking, "Underutilized . . . for what, by what, or compared to what?" (*HF*, 61). Sam is quick to recognize that the doctors' terms describing Lucy are nothing more than "labels" that have little to do with her. Gus, too, knows that language can be misused, recalling that no one protested when the government seized their lands for the reservoir because, as he says, " 'eminent domain' is a big fancy term" that "reeked of some kind of celestial approval," as if "God ordered it, not the state legislature. Sort of like Manifest Destiny" (150). And when Sam travels back in time to witness Lucy's funeral 50 years earlier, he reflects that the words of the minister are "meaningless—wooden sounds that knocked and banged like an unlatched gate in the wind" (230).

Organized religion, treated here with devastating humor, also comes under fire. When Gus explains his unorthodox beliefs, Sam sees "more belief in the old man's gaze than he had in a year of Sundays in the church" back in Indiana (*HF*, 67). Gus seems to have inherited his unconventional perspective from his father, who was "merciless" about what he saw as the "religious fanatics" in the family. Gus finds his father's position amusing: although he is "not one for organized religion," he would be the "last ever to call a Congregationalist a fanatic. Hell," he exclaims, "you practically have to take a pulse on them during worship" (153).

The novel is structured in four parts: "An Accidental Wilderness," "The Lost Valley," "The Lost Girl," and "Reclamation." The first section is longest, more than half the book; the succeeding sections grow increasingly short, with the last section only a few pages. The chapters within each section are also short. The combined effect is a story that unfolds slowly at first, then picks up its tempo, moving more and more rapidly as it draws to a finish, its accelerating pace analogous to Lucy's growing awareness of the external world. The settings usually change between chapters, but with smooth transitions. When Lucy murmurs "Home free" at the close of one chapter, for example, the next chapter begins with a question from Gus: "Lucy talking pretty good now, Sam?" (*HF*, 145). These connections create an almost visual fade; this, coupled with Lasky's rich descriptions of landscape and wildlife, give the novel a cinematic quality.

Home Free is the first of Lasky's young adult novels to use fantasy. Lasky's fantasy in her fiction is of a very particular nature. "I've never been into high fantasy with witches and warlocks," she says. Instead, her fantasy elements appear as logical extensions of the natural world. In this novel, she has anchored the fantasy—communication with eagles and time travel—in scientific fact drawn from her own knowledge of birds and physics. Lasky's interest in eagles stemmed from a film that her husband, a professional photographer, made about the birds' extraordinary capabilities. Lasky's own knowledge of the subject is very much in evidence here: The realistic sections of the novel offer abundant information about the physiology of eagles, particularly their phenomenal eyesight and flight abilities. Ilirah is presented in such careful detail that when she begins to "speak" with precise movements of her head and eyes, "slivers of motion" (*HF*, 161), the communication appears convincingly avian. One might assume that Lasky harbors a deep affection and respect for these birds, but she confesses that she is no bird fancier and that her daughter's cockatoo frightens her. "I can't stand to go into the room when she has it out of the cage," she says.

Lasky's approach to the time travel segment also incorporates science. Early in the book Sam's journey is foreshadowed when he recalls talking with his father about the relativity of time, introducing the notion that time is not fixed but flexible. The idea of time travel, with its promise of exploring the past, intrigues Lasky. "For me, the ultimate fantasy involves those time warps that take you back to familiar worlds that your world has grown out of." Her characteristic interest in the past has invested the time travel episode of *Home Free* with substantial information about the shameful child labor practices of nineteenth-century New England mills.

Sam journeys with Ilirah back to the creation of the universe, then forward through the evolution of entire species and, finally, to Lucy's town of 50 years ago. The travel through time seems to hinge on "a strong joining of mind and consciousness," a "super or cosmic awareness," a concept that intrigues several of Lasky's adolescent protagonists. Like them, Sam is responsive to the mysteries of the cosmos, often scanning the night sky in search of constellations. As he wonders about his place in the universe, Lasky injects another recurring theme: the insignificance of human beings in relationship to the infinity of the galaxies.

Although the first two-thirds of the book are highly realistic, there are early hints of a supernatural element to prepare the reader for what is coming. Still, despite the care with which Lasky shifts from realism to fantasy, it is difficult to suspend disbelief while reading this strand of the story. Some of the earlier clues that point to Lucy's past life heighten interest and suspense; for example, Lucy's fright at seeing her reflection in the water foreshadows her drowning 50 years earlier. But others are simply confusing: Why does Lucy appear to have a nictitating membrane, the "third eyelid" peculiar to birds? Is she, in fact, an eagle? Granted, the fantasy—especially the time travel element—provides a fascinating narrative, the descriptive passages distinguished by the lyricism so typical of Lasky's prose. However, it seems appended to the earlier story, not integrated with it, a deus ex machina that handily (and implausibly) explains and cures Lucy's autism. As a review in *Booklist* noted, "The introduction of the fantasy element comes too late and seems to belong in another book."[7]

Other reviewers voiced similar objections. "Lasky is really writing three books here, a psychological novel, a time fantasy, and realistic fiction about human and natural cycles," noted the *Bulletin of the Center for Children's Books*. "Each story is itself fascinating but doesn't always blend with the others."[8] *School Library Journal*, while praising the characters as "extremely well drawn" and the style as "often lyrical," said bluntly that "there are too many elements, and the story loses both energy and clarity through the fantasy."[9]

There are also unnecessary shifts in the narrative point of view, a recurring problem in Lasky's fiction. Told in the third person, the narrative viewpoint is mostly Sam's in Part I, with a letter from Sam to his grandparents written in the mandatory first person. Occasionally in the early chapters the viewpoint switches to Phillipa and Gus but without intruding on the narrative flow. More jarring are the shifts in the later sections: A scene in the Quabbin wilderness with Sam asleep in his tent is suddenly rendered from an eagle's point of view, and in the time travel sequence, the viewpoint jumps from Sam's to Lucy's to that of minor characters such as Lucy's aunt or cousin, or to an omniscient narrator, who fills in the history of Lucy's early life.

However flawed, *Home Free* nonetheless stands as what *Voice of Youth Advocates* called "a majestic story of people coming to terms with the fragile balance of life that is needed for living on this planet."[10] Readers who follow Sam's long and sometimes painful journey will exult in his triumphs and in his discovery of that elusive place called "home."

Pageant

Both Birdie and Sam might well envy the loving, stable family of Sarah Benjamin, the protagonist of the novel *Pageant,* published in 1986. Sarah is the cherished younger daughter of upper-middle-class parents living in Indianapolis in the early 1960s. Her father, Alfred, is an eminent plastic surgeon and loving husband; her mother, Shirley, is an energetic community activist who battles censorship, delivers Meals on Wheels, and has returned to school as a business major, earning straight As. They both find Sarah "adorable" and demonstrate infinite parental patience. Marla, Sarah's older sister, is a musically gifted prodigy, who provides steady—and steadying—support to Sarah, helping her with pesky conjugations of French verbs and serving as a sounding board for Sarah's problems. They are an ideal family, interchangeable in many ways with Rachel's family in *The Night Journey:* They are cultured, affectionate, prosperous—and Jewish.

This last characteristic is what sets the story on its course. Sarah attends Stuart Hall, a private school affiliated with the Episcopal Church, because her friends are students there. Although the school "was not supposed to be religious,"[11] Sarah and her classmates spend 8 to 10 hours a week each November and December rehearsing a nativity pageant for the school's Christmas program. Sarah plays a shepherd, a role won by default: Her unruly dark hair has disqualified her as an angel, a role that the headmistress envisions only for blond, blue-eyed girls. In the environment of Stuart Hall, Sarah is an outsider.

Pageant is Lasky's most autobiographical novel. Like Sarah, Lasky grew up in a devoted and affectionate Jewish family. Marla is much like Lasky's older sister, Martha, with whom she enjoyed a very close relationship. Her school experiences also parallel Sarah's in many ways: She attended a private Episcopal school, where she was one of three Jewish students, spending several years playing a shepherd in the school Christmas pageant because of her dark complexion.[12] And she, too, learned ancient history from a teacher who warned about "creeping Orientalism," a reference to the dangers posed by people with dark skin and tilted eyes. The novel "just kind of tumbled out," she says.

Pageant addresses the theme of prejudice from a somewhat different angle than Lasky's earlier novels. Sarah encounters not deliberately cruel acts of persecution such as those portrayed in *The Night Journey* and *Prank* but belittling attitudes about minorities, a casual tyranny of the white Christian majority. At times Sarah feels her difference keenly. At Stuart Hall, thinking back on all the blond angels in the pageant, she finds it "slightly disturbing to think that there was neither a role on the stage nor in heaven for her 'type' " (*Pageant*, 93). On her first date with the handsome, "cool" Ethan Johnson, who is not Jewish, she has "this lurking feeling that his asking her was some sort of mistake" (156), and she is uncomfortably aware that the color of her dress, bluish, rhymes with her religion. She is also sensitive to racial prejudice, discomfited by the statues of "little black boys" that populate her neighborhood (7), and she recognizes the racism inherent in the school's official stance on certain matters, for instance the headmistress's ban on Indian-style headbands.

However, as sensitive as she is to these displays of prejudice, she fails to recognize the subtle pressures that threaten to erode her own distinctive heritage. Sarah and her family practice their religion by celebrating the major Jewish holidays with traditional Jewish prayers and food, but they also mark Christmas by purchasing a "small, discreet tree appropriate for a reformed Jewish family" (*Pageant*, 149), oblivious to the oxymoronic linking of "appropriate" with "Jewish." The tree-trimming scene is presented so idyllically, as a "perfect" and "exquisitely happy" evening, that the reader is surely intended to agree with Sarah's mother that the Christmas tree is "a very nice idea" (155). But the family's Jewish identity seems compromised.

As for Sarah, she knows no Hebrew (instead, she's studying French and Latin), attends synagogue only on major holidays (and then reluctantly), claims she would rather serve in the ancient temple of Vesta (about which she's learning at school) than be bat mitzvahed. Nonetheless, she objects to being called an "assimilated Jew," explaining in an autobiographical essay written for her French class that "the word *assimilated* suggests a diluted Jew." She insists that she "would be the same Jew in Israel, in Russia, in Italy, in England, in China" (*Pageant*, 87). But her essay indicates exactly how "assimilated" she is—how little she knows about her religion and about the effects of a dominant culture upon it.

Positioned as she is as a Jew (albeit an assimilated one) on the margins of a WASPish society, Sarah struggles to define herself. Like Meribah, she realizes that she is being defined by others, in terms of other people: "her father; her sister; even, in a way, her aunt" (*Pageant*, 85–86). But who is she? The cumulative events of the novel, which cover three years of Sarah's life, lead her to an answer. The novel is structured in four parts, and each section opens with a rehearsal for the nativity pageant in successive years—1960, 1961, 1962, 1963. The nation's political climate during this time, from Kennedy's election and rumblings of the war in Vietnam to Kennedy's assassination, provides a backdrop for Sarah's own story.

She is one of only three Kennedy supporters in the solidly Republican school, and in the opening scene, set in early November before the 1960 presidential election, she is soundly rebuked for wearing a Kennedy button on her burnoose. This is but the first of several attempts by the school administration to restrict Sarah's actions. She is not one to accede easily to such limitations, and her sometimes poignant, often comic responses to authority and narrow-mindedness help her define herself on her own terms.

Like many of Lasky's young adult protagonists, she wants to be "apart" from her family but not "alone." She needs their support and love at the same time that she needs independence from them. This is a paradox common to adolescents and a source of considerable internal conflict for Sarah. Her longing for independence intensifies when her Aunt Hattie, a successful impresario from New York, comes to live with the family while she recovers from cancer surgery. Hattie moves in the day after Marla leaves for Wellesley College, so Sarah faces a double adjustment: She has lost Marla's companionship and now must share her home (and bathroom) with Aunt Hattie instead of with her sister. Sharing space with Hattie, "who trilled hygienic aphorisms over running bathwater" (*Pageant,* 49), is difficult. Hattie borrows her barrettes and cologne without asking, offers unwanted advice on her appearance, and tries to manage Sarah's life as if her niece were one of her clients.

After Sarah triggers an explosive quarrel with Hattie at the dinner table, her father gives her a lesson in "family physics":

> Opposites attract. We are all as a family a bunch of positive and negative charges and therefore we all hang together. This is the nuclear family. . . . And you in your insensitivity and rudeness have thrown in an extra negative charge: You have upset the balance—the bonding. (64)

His explanation provides yet another answer to Birdie's question "What is a family?" by emphasizing the mutual responsibility of family members to each other.

Sarah patches up her relationship with Hattie, and her growing recognition of her aunt's abilities signals an increased maturity, but her life tilts increasingly downhill. Her best friend, Elaine, now has a steady boyfriend and is more interested in primping than in exchanging confidences with Sarah. Sarah's date with Ethan ends disastrously when he makes a racial slur about blacks in the same moment that he makes an unwelcome sexual overture. Sarah is equally offended by both actions and walks home through the snow rather than remain in the car.

This episode is the first of several in which sex impinges on her world. Although Sarah understands what takes place physically during the sexual act, she does not yet comprehend its emotional aspect, and her eventual acceptance of sex as part of male-female relationships marks another aspect of her initiation into the adult world. While studying *Idylls of the King* in her literature class, she learns to her dismay that Sir Lancelot and Guinevere, whom she has viewed as idealized lovers, were "doing it." It is, she thinks, "as if sex had become some sort of joke and . . . she simply did not find the punch line as funny as the rest of the world" (*Pageant*, 142). Later, she is stunned to learn that her lab partner in physics has dropped out of school to have a baby. "To imagine Emily going all the way was almost impossible" for Sarah, who is unable to reconcile her image of the unattractive and studious Emily with sexual behavior (178).

Sarah succumbs to gloom. To raise her spirits, her understanding parents take her to Disneyland. However, she finds its artificiality disconcerting, and the racially condescending remarks of a guide on a "jungle" tour only magnify her malaise. Back at school, she receives a final blow when the school censors her science project designed to gauge racial attitudes, refusing to encourage independent inquiry or acknowledge that the mind-set among some of its faculty and students might contribute to social problems in the outside world.

Rehearsing for the Christmas pageant for the fourth time, Sarah calculates that she has spent 116 hours over the last three years in "a heap of sleeping shepherds" (*Pageant*, 195). She has read in one of her father's medical journals that all mammals are allotted the same number of breaths and heartbeats in a lifetime, although the pace varies. The question, then, becomes "How did one spend those beats and breaths?" (195). She feels as if her life is going nowhere; "nothing had changed" (179). During a November rehearsal in 1963, when she hears the familiar line "Shepherds, shake off your drowsy sleep," she walks off the stage, then drives to New York to see Marla, now studying music at Julliard.

Her flight catapults her into further complications. She hears over the car radio the cataclysmic news that Kennedy has been assassinated, and once in New York she finds that Marla is living with a young man, an Israeli cellist and fellow student. Devastated by the discovery that Marla is no longer a virgin (sex again!), she flees to the New York apartment of famed dancer Serge Vronsky, one of Hattie's friends and clients. He helps her understand that her reaction to Marla's living arrangement is sorrow over losing the innocence of her childhood world. Eventually, her concerned parents allow her to finish high school in Manhattan, living with Aunt Hattie, and her father concedes that she has "learned the lesson in nuclear family physics" (219).

The lesson is clear. Family, as constructed in *Pageant*, is a generous source of strength but a stern creditor: It provides its members with unwavering love and understanding but demands that they return the same, not always an easy obligation to fulfill. Sarah learns, too, that family is part of each person's identity—but not the whole of it, as the final pages of the novel demonstrate. The brief closing chapter summarizes "significant dates" in Sarah's post–Stuart Hall life and follows her to Sierre Leone, where she is a member of the Peace Corps, finally "part of a real pageant" on Kennedy's New Frontier (*Pageant*, 221). Ultimately Sarah has defined herself, creating a niche "apart" from her family but enacting the values she has learned from them: She has found her own way to emulate her parents, "to do something serious" (102).

Sarah is among Lasky's most privileged young characters, sheltered in many ways from the harsh realities that confront some of her other adolescent protagonists. Still, she finds that negotiating the passage from childhood to adulthood is no easy matter. Marla reassures her by saying, "Things get better.... You get more control. You get more power over things" (*Pageant*, 141), but at the time Marla's words provide small comfort to Sarah, who is acutely conscious that by virtue of her politics, religion, gender, and age she has very little power. "Power [is] important," she realizes, and with this insight she understands why her mother "liked reading about corporate power and Marla liked living on her own in New York and she herself hated being a shepherd" (141).

The trajectory of Sarah's development traces her growing empowerment. She first responds to her feelings of impotence with rebellion. For example, when the school issues a restrictive new code for lunchroom behavior, Sarah inks a patently absurd rule on the official document, determined to be "no one's puppet." With this act of defiance comes a new sensation: "the warm glow, the first glimmerings, of the guerrilla in her soul" (*Pageant*, 129). She learns that she can act independently. She helps to rescue one of Aunt Hattie's artists, an immigrant violinist stranded in a snowstorm, and brings the young woman back to her home. She also learns that her gender need not position her in a helpless role. When Ethan parks his car on a secluded road and offers her some liquor, she first tries to refuse politely, wondering "how to say no without offending him" (159). But she is sufficiently outraged by his subsequent actions that she tells him bluntly that he is a "creep," rejecting both his advances and the code of behavior dictating that women should not offend men or express their feelings directly.

These steps lead to her ultimate declaration of independence. After fleeing to New York, she tells her parents that she wants to remain there for "awhile." Her mother replies that Sarah has "her whole life" for such decisions, but Sarah is not easily deterred. Conscious of time surging forward, of her own heart spending its measured allotment of beats, she knows that some decisions cannot be postponed. That is, she has earned a more adult status and is determined to claim it. "I can't be a shepherd anymore," she insists (*Pageant*, 213). She knows that returning to Indianapolis won't "fix" anything, an insight that Marla corroborates: "The important point is that neither you nor I are babies anymore" (215). The closing events of the novel, in which Sarah graduates from high school and defers her admission to Cornell University to join the Peace Corps, confirms Marla's judgment.

Sarah is a literary sister of Lasky's other YA protagonists: She is highly idealistic, with a ready sympathy for the oppressed (she is a "principled person," Hattie tells her), a spunky, creative problem solver. Like Birdie and Sam, she is well acquainted with a range of literature (from Shakespeare to James Whitcomb Riley) and shares with them a talent for writing, even winning the French essay contest. She also shares with her predecessors a cosmic awareness that however large her own life and problems loom, they are relatively insignificant. Like Birdie, she despairs of anything in her life ever changing but recognizes the necessity for change if she is to realize her dreams and ambitions. Although her story is set more than a century after Meribah's, she, too, sees herself as a "pioneer," a "lone voyager" along Kennedy's New Frontier. Her stint with the Peace Corps provides a fitting close to her journey.

Sarah's religious views seem to mirror Lasky's own. Sarah writes in her autobiographical essay, "I never feel close to God in a building.... I don't like organized religion. I prefer religion in private with my family. I prefer to pray alone in a low voice" (*Pageant,* 87). Lasky says, "I don't like organized religion and never have. I always hated going to Temple. I've only felt spiritual when I've been in nature. I don't have to be in a building saying a prayer in unison."

Lasky says she couldn't have written this novel without some emotional distance from her own experiences. "If I had written it when I was younger," she says, "I wouldn't have been able to see much humor in it." As is, the wry wit often found in Lasky's work enlivens the novel, stemming as it does from the usually affectionate but sometimes abrasive interactions of her characters. When Sarah tells her mother that the headmistress chooses only blonds to play the angels, Marla adds, "I actually don't dare imagine what [her] requirements for the Virgin Mary are" (*Pageant,* 15). To Hattie's remark that her skin is so dry that she is "virtually a Mojave Desert," Sarah whispers, "What about Death Valley?" (62).

The style, too, is characteristic of Lasky. The lyricism of her earlier novels is in evidence here, particularly in passages that convey aural images. As Sarah listens to her sister playing a Chopin etude, "The sounds came shimmering and fragile. Like great bubbles they floated through the house" (*Pageant,* 20). Later, after braving a fierce snowstorm to rescue Lieba, a violinist and one of Hattie's clients, she hears Lieba play her violin on the bus ride home, "a soft, distant glow of sound. Slowly it filled the bus, first with the warm, burnished tone of a dark-hued adagio, then with the silvery quick strokes of an allegro" (112).

Lasky's precise images often convey in this novel not only the sensory detail itself but the emotional content of the moment. When Sarah rejects her date's sexual advance, she speaks his name "like a flat, broad cooked noodle" (*Pageant*, 159). The tranquillity of a snowfall is described as being like a pointillist painting, consisting of millions of dots that envelop familiar buildings in "a gossamer web of magic and silence" (102).

There are also several instances of mimetic fiction, a staple of Lasky's work: Sarah writes letters to Marla, composes an autobiographical essay for her French class, and—in a perfect facsimile of high school academic discourse—gives directions for participating in her science project.

The novel, written in the third person, is seen almost entirely through Sarah's eyes. The controlled point of view, which avoids the jarring shifts of some of Lasky's earlier novels, is a definite strength, as is the tighter narrative focus. There are, however, some digressive episodes. A discussion about the ancient Battle of Salamis reveals a teacher's bigotry when she ignorantly refers to "oriental despotism"; another, about *Idylls of the Kings,* exposes a teacher's misty and misguided view of King Arthur, which is juxtaposed with Sarah's more mature understanding of the text. A lengthy episode centered around Serge Vronsky's performance in *Sleeping Beauty* opens Sarah's eyes to the variety of women in the world. Although each incident contributes to Sarah's development, they seem long for the slender insights they yield.

This novel earned praise from the start. Lasky's editor, Meredith Charpentier, responded enthusiastically to an early draft. "Such a good book," she wrote, "such humor and power.... I actually reread parts for pleasure, and that's definitely a no-no when editing under time pressure."[13] It also garnered enthusiastic reviews that singled out Lasky's skillful handling of humor for special praise. Hazel Rochman wrote that the story is told "with warmth and wit," a response echoed by Alba Quinones Endicott: "The story of Sarah's changes and development during a unique time in the political history of the United States is told with humor, sensitivity, and compassion."[14] Denise M. Wilms, writing in *Booklist,* found that "the scenes unfold with wit and style.

Lasky's sharp sense of humor and ear for dialogue and repartee are a pleasure to behold. Her portrait of Sarah's family is warm and welcome."[15]

Lasky has also written a family novel for adults, *The Widow of Oz*. Dorothy Silver, its protagonist, is, at 52 and newly widowed, at a juncture in her life, and her development parallels in many ways the path of Sarah's coming-of-age. Dorothy's mother named her for the character of the same name in *The Wizard of Oz*, an identification she resists. Her own life has been carefully scripted, tornado-free. Then her cardiologist husband dies suddenly of a heart attack, shortly after he has persuaded Dorothy to sell their comfortable suburban home and move into an upscale condo in Boston. For the first time, the events of Dorothy's life appear random and unscripted.

Like Sarah, Dorothy discovers a guerrilla in her soul. She finds that she likes the unfinished look of her condo, whose walls are unpainted and whose floor is uncarpeted. "It seemed impermanent and ready for action,"[16] an objective correlative of Dorothy's emotional state. Defying convention, she covers the floors with spattered painters' cloths and creates a dining table from a long board supported by two sawhorses.

Her relationships with her adult children change, much as—conversely—Sarah's relationships with her parents change, for Sarah and Dorothy are forging identities that separate them from their accustomed familial roles. Dorothy takes charge of her stock investments, exchanges long letters with her son's primatologist girlfriend (whose detailed accounts of her work in Nairobi with a troop of baboons look ahead to the observations of real-life Allison Jolly of Lasky's nonfiction children's book *Shadows in the Dawn*), buys a cottage on an unfashionable island off the Maine coast, and makes new friends.

As she moves past grief, she engages in "a new story of her own making," discovering, as she says, that "I am very different from the person that I ever imagined myself to be—ever!" (*WO*, 141, 171). Learning to sail, she finds a navigational metaphor for her life: "Instead of being buffeted by the maverick winds, she conjured them" (174). Then, in the closing pages, when she finds herself on the bay in a fog that seems to recalls her earlier state of widowhood, "lost . . . without reference," as if "she had slipped her gravitational orbit," she regains her bearings and sails "smartly for home" (280, 282). Like Sarah, the home for which she sails is not the home from which she departed, but she has found a way of making peace with her past while looking toward the future.

This is a thoughtful novel that takes an unflinching look at how widowhood changes a woman's life. It includes certain of Lasky's trademarks—literary references, vivid imagery, encyclopedic information (about primate behavior in this instance), and a range of colorful characters, but Lasky views it as significantly distinct from her other novels. "It's more inward," she says. Critics responded favorably. *Publishers Weekly* called it a "thoughtful, appealing novel." Denise Perry Donavin, writing for *Booklist,* said the book was "[a] lovely, cheering story of a woman's blossoming self-awareness."[17]

Conclusion

Although Lasky's contemporary adolescent protagonists share with the characters in her historical fiction a vigorous idealism and quick intelligence, the former are products of a different culture. Freed from worry about matters of physical survival, these adolescents are more self-absorbed, more concerned about their emotional well-being and about relationships with friends and family. They are occasionally sulky; Birdie and Sarah in particular fret in typical adolescent fashion over appearance and popularity. All resist cultural pressures that dictate how they should behave as young men or women; instead, each finds a unique space in the world where she or he can translate lofty aspirations into useful realities.

They all learn that they are, inextricably, part of a "family," of a heritage that is, variably, a source of strength or vulnerability. They also learn that they must resolve their own ambivalences about their parents and siblings before they can gain a secure foothold in the adult world. All encounter loneliness and self-doubt on their way to maturity, and they confront issues that loom gigantic in the face of their untried youth. In overcoming these obstacles, they measure themselves against those individuals whom they perceive as "heroes"—parents, adult friends, historical and political figures—and strive to emulate the best of what they have observed. In so doing, they provide models for readers traveling the uneven road from childhood to maturity, demonstrating that, given a generous spirit and a caring heart, the journey can be exciting and even triumphant.

6. Danger: Zealots at Work

Lasky often alludes in her fiction to what she sees as the ineffectual, even dangerous aspects of organized religion, but in many of her YA novels that issue is peripheral to others. *Memoirs of a Bookbat* and *Beyond the Burning Time,* both published in 1994, reverse that emphasis. Although their respective stories are separated by 300 years and each echoes many of Lasky's favorite themes, they take as their primary focus the problem of thought control as exercised by zealous religious forces. "Organized religion gives too many easy answers," Lasky says. In these two novels she dramatizes the dangers of doctrinaire beliefs that provide "easy"—but specious—answers to complex questions.

Memoirs of a Bookbat

Harper Jessup is the bookbat of the title. She loves to read but insists she is not a bookworm, a term that reminds her of "some mindless creature living on mold underground."[1] Rather, she sees herself as a bookbat, "soaring and swooping through the night, skimming across the treetops" as she reads, the books showing her the way through a dark forest (*MB*, 31–32). The "forest" has taken root in her parents' newfound religious fundamentalism, and the darkness is one of proliferating strictures consisting of what she may and may not do. Many of the "may nots" involve her choice of books.

The idea for this novel was sparked by Lasky's son, Max, to whom the book is dedicated. He was reading an article about a family who had tried to remove from the school library any book that involved horror or the occult. A fan of Anne Rice, Max was dismayed. "Boy," he said, "I'd be dead meat if I had been born into this family." Lasky began to wonder "what would happen to a kid like that. He'd die, just expire." And Harper Jessup, a "kid like that," was born.

Harper does not expire, but when the reader first meets her, she is running away from home. This novel, like *Beyond the Divide* and *True North,* opens late in the plot, when Harper is 14. It then circles back seven years to trace the events leading to the first chapter. Written in the first person (the only one of Lasky's YA novels rendered from this viewpoint), the story is enlivened by Harper's intelligent, sometimes acerbic voice.

Harper's problems begin when her father, Hank, loses his job and the family moves into a shabby trailer court. Hank is drinking heavily, and at night Harper can overhear her parents quarreling. Then her mother, Beth, takes Hank to a fundamentalist prayer group, which they join; the quarreling and the drinking stop, Hank finds maintenance work with the church, and the homey smell of vanilla from Beth's baked goods once more fills their home. On the surface things seem better, but almost immediately Harper feels as if she, like Goldilocks, has "stumbled into the wrong house, into some place [she] didn't belong" (*MB*, 21).

Through the prayer group, her parents become deeply involved in an organization called Family Action for Christian Education (F.A.C.E.). Hank proves himself such an eloquent spokesman for the group's "anti-humanism" position on public education that soon the Jessups are on the road in a sleek Roadmaster mobile home (courtesy of F.A.C.E.) to combat "blasphemy" in the school curriculum. They are, Harper's mother tells her, "migrants for God" (5).

But Harper's sense of displacement grows. Her parents become suddenly suspicious of her trips to the library, of the books she is reading. The bookbat in her knows that books are as important to her survival as food and air, and she begins to find ways to circumvent her parents' censorship. Like Sarah Benjamin of *Pageant,* she discovers the "guerrilla" in her soul. She thinks of herself as a Brer Rabbit, too little and too vulnerable for "open rebellion" (*MB*, 34), an insurgent who must rely on wit—and deception—to outsmart the powerful Brer Foxes of F.A.C.E.

Because the family rarely stays in any one place for more than a month, Harper's friends are mostly the characters she meets through her reading. She is delighted to discover the services of interlibrary lending, which keep her well supplied with books. She hides them, disguised in schoolbook covers, in a cubby she has discovered in the closet of her Roadmaster bedroom. Finally, in Tennessee, she makes real friends, three other girls who, like Harper, have been sent to the library during science period because their parents disapprove of the school textbooks that teach evolutionary theory. For the first time, she is able to share her most urgent and personal concerns: training bras and sanitary pads. She cannot approach her mother about these subjects—although sex itself as a source of misconduct and perversion is a frequent topic among her parents and the other church activists. Then the Jessups move on, and Harper is on her own again.

But only briefly. In California, she meets Gray Willette in the science fiction section of the public library. Gray is different from the other people she has met along the way; neither he nor his family has any connection with the Jessups' church, and the Willettes are warm, open, and accepting. In Gray she has found a friend with a sense of humor who shares her fascination with the night sky. He steers her to his favorite sci-fi writers, and she helps cure his gerbil of mange. (Harper has gained some expertise with gerbils because the libraries across the country that she has frequented keep gerbils in the children's reading section.[2]) Gray's house becomes Harper's home away from home.

Lasky uses Harper's growing estrangement from her family to make several points about religious zealots. First, they are immoderately self-righteous. Reverend Dan LePage, head of F.I.S.T. (Families Involved in Saving Traditional Values, the organization that is funding F.A.C.E.), is so assured of his moral superiority that he boasts of daily "chats" with God on the censorship issue. He even quotes the Lord's response: "Dan, these are your missionaries. These are the good Christians who will help make the people understand the devil in those pages" (*MB*, 90). Harper is skeptical: "This man didn't have just the Lord's private phone number, but his appointment book, too" (90).

Lasky's mystery for adults, *Mortal Words,* paints a similar picture of religious zealots but presents them in an even less favorable light than does *Memoirs.* Here they are not only zealous censors and greedy hypocrites but psychopaths who will murder to protect their turf. This novel grew out of Lasky's one experience with censorship. She had just finished a presentation on *Traces of Life* and was surrounded by people who had approached her to say how much they enjoyed her speech. "Then, I felt this claw on my shoulder . . . and someone sort of spun me around. I was shocked to see how small she was and that she was so properly dressed. She was just livid and said, 'That might be your religion, but it's not mine. Your book will never be on my library shelf" (Donavin, 246). Lasky was too shocked to respond, but she began thinking: what if someone in her situation were murdered? *Mortal Words* pushes the moral smugness of religious zealots to its ultimate extremes.

Although the zealots do not resort to murder in *Memoirs,* their narrow moral certitude inevitably results in other kinds of damage, generating distrust, even hatred, of those who think differently. Harper observes that her parents have become suspicious of everyone who is not aligned with their organization. The suspicion and hatred are contagious, infecting even young children. Nowhere is this point made more forcefully than in a scene involving Harper's younger sister Weesie and Weesie's friend Cindy, also a daughter of religious activists. As the two little girls play with their Barbie dolls, Cindy remarks that "we hate, hate, hate" Catholics and Jews and niggers (*MB,* 130). Later, Weesie and Cindy write a nasty letter to "JEWdy Blume" and try to recruit a classmate for their Jesus Club by threatening her with hellfire. Dismayed at what is happening to her sister, Harper tries to reason with her, but she comes to realize, sadly, that Weesie's mind is "up for grabs," that she is "owned."

Suspicion of outsiders leads the zealots to see evil everywhere. As Harper observes, "These grown-ups had more fears and worries than you could shake a stick at" (*MB,* 39). They are afraid of anyone and anything they cannot control—public education, the U.S. government, normal adolescent development. Control, in fact, is key: the leaders are more concerned with power than with piety. The Reverend Dan LePage addresses Harper as "young lady," putting her in her place much as Birdie's parents do by calling her "missy," but Harper comes to see that everyone in LePage's organization—male and female, young and old—is a "young lady" to him. A star of F.I.S.T.'s cable television network, with more Hollywood than holiness in his tactics, he "whittles" his followers down to size with his moral smugness and spellbinding power. His opinions are their opinions.

The authoritarian methods of F.A.C.E. and F.I.S.T. allow no room for questioning or independent thought. A key scene occurs when Harper's father remarks that LePage is a "latter-day Custer" (*MB*, 97), and Harper replies that Custer was a "total creep." For the reader, there is sly irony in her response, as Lasky's adroit and derisive characterization of LePage leaves no doubt that the reverend is also a total creep. But to Hank Jessup, both are heroes, and he reacts with consternation to the idea that Harper has "interpreted" the facts she's learned at school (Custer graduated at the bottom of his West Point class, wore perfume, and broke treaties with the Sioux). Interpretation, of course, signifies independent, critical thinking, and Hank takes Harper's explanation as evidence that "Satan can make inroads into a young mind" (99). Significantly, he uses military metaphors to express what are supposedly Christian ideals: "Your brain must become a fortress against these ideas; your heart must be an arsenal" (57).

Unwilling to surrender either her brain or her heart, Harper is left with few choices. Either she can openly resist, or she can resort to duplicity. She chooses the latter, beginning with minor acts of subterfuge, enjoying her Brer Rabbit victories but sometimes feeling that she has betrayed herself. Her evasions escalate to the point where she lies constantly, practicing deceit until she becomes "good at it" (*MB,* 176). She even pretends to be the "best Christian of the whole lot" (41). Lasky's implication is clear. The rigid thought control exacted by religious zealotry can provoke evasions and dishonesty in those who resist its doctrines.

Hank and Beth, on the other hand, seem to welcome the strong direction LePage and his associates provide. "Not everyone needs to be the boss" (*MB*, 133), says Harper's mother, who willingly follows the advice of a fundamentalist friend on everything from shopping and makeup to religion. Harper observes that all the rules and admonitions make "life easy" for her parents (131), much as the easy "answers" in Holly Springs in *Beyond the Divide* make life secure for those who accept them—but difficult for those who do not.

As F.A.C.E. and its parent organization push their agenda, the stakes increase. What begins as an attempt to censor specific books in school libraries broadens into a campaign to control educational curriculum across the country, blurring the boundaries between church and state. Finally, the group mounts a crusade against abortion.

Harper grows more and more uncomfortable with her double life. Where—and to whom—does she belong? Like the protagonists of *Prank, Home Free,* and *Pageant,* she wonders about the nature of "family." She is on a collision course with her parents, who make her feel like a stranger in her own home and suspect her of doing "dark and hidden" things with Gray (*MB*, 135). The one relative with whom she feels a familial bond is her maternal grandmother, Gammy, but her father severs connections between the two after he hears Gammy sing what he calls a "heathen" folk song to the moon.

After giving troubled thought to the dual questions of family and belonging, Harper articulates an answer:

> To belong did not mean ownership.... The "be" syllable was about existence: "to be" yourself ... in a special place that no one else could occupy within your family except you. The "long" part was about the heart, a place in the heart where a family met and lived together.... They longed for each other. (*MB*, 161–62)

By Harper's definition, she does not belong to or with her own family.

Harper's parents see the issue differently. When they learn about a bridge-building contest at school that Harper and Gray have won with their Apocalypse Bridge (a "revelatory" bridge in terms of its construction, Gray explains on television), they label the project "blasphemous" and forbid Harper to associate with "that boy" anymore. Harper protests that her parents cannot control her whole life; her mother retorts, "You belong to us, Harper" (*MB*, 170). And when Harper resists participating in an antiabortion demonstration, her father ignores her protests. He says to her mother, "We are going as a family to this march. There is no choice here. She belongs with us" (186). By her parents' definition, family is a hierarchical arrangement in which children are not individuals but possessions.

Harper gives in to her family's wishes but quarrels with Gray over her decision, then regrets her harsh words to him. She has played "fast and loose" with a friendship, much, she reflects, as Huckleberry Finn did with the slave Jim. She imagines a little person in her heart or her brain, beating its fists and stomping its feet, someone she recognizes: "Her name was Jim. And she wanted her freedom" (*MB*, 196). Harper gains that freedom with Gray's help by running away to Gammy's. She travels light: a change of clothing, a letter from a favorite author, a feather that her bird Wingo has molted, and a vanilla bean. Although Harper feels as if she is on the opposite side of an immense canyon from her family, she still values the best of what her mother (by far the more sympathetically portrayed parent) has given her, just as Meribah in *Beyond the Divide* fondly remembers the color gray.

An epilogue with a long letter from Gray closes Harper's story: Gammy's minister has supported Harper's decision to stay with her grandmother; Gray is coming to visit, and both Harper and Gray have been invited to the home of one of their favorite authors—a piece of particularly good fortune, since books and authors are central to Harper's life and to the novel. In fact, fully one-third of the novel's chapter titles refer either to the titles or characters of other literary texts.

Harper's love of literature aligns her with Lasky's other adolescent protagonists, most of whom are avid readers. Harper not only loves to read but takes her moral direction from fictional characters, in particular Brer Rabbit, Judy Blume's adolescents, and

Huckleberry Finn. A turning point for Harper comes when she recognizes, like Huckleberry, that you can't pray a lie: she cannot pretend to embrace values that she doesn't accept. Harper is also linked to Lasky's other YA characters by her spunky independence, thoughtful intelligence, and sturdy moral sense. Like her contemporary counterparts, she cares deeply about having close friends, and her sometimes self-mocking sense of humor helps her, as it has helped her predecessors, keep things in perspective. Like all of Lasky's adolescent protagonists, both historical and contemporary, she is fascinated by the mysteries of nature and finds planet Earth an exciting place. Too, she is enthralled and consoled by the beauty of the night sky; at one point, feeling "weak and punched out," she finds it very comforting to know that she and Gray, Huckleberry, and "long ago, Mr. Twain, had all looked up and seen the same sky" (*MB,* 183). She also shares her perspective on her place in the universe with other Lasky adolescents: Harper understands that, in the phrase that marks almost all of Lasky's novels, she occupies a small planet in a minor galaxy.

Typical, too, is the lively dialogue and vivid imagery that serve here to sharpen characterization and setting. Beth's friend has a "tight little voice, like stitches ripping"; Harper watches a violent storm "peel back the night and lay bare the bones of heaven" (*MB,* 36, 204).

Memoirs received mixed reviews. Those favorable to the book, such as Lesley Farmer, writing for the *Book Report,* praised its "interesting plot" and a family conflict that "rings true."[3] The *Horn Book Guide* said that "Lasky tells a good story," and an article about multiple literacies in the *Reading Teacher* noted that "the book speaks powerfully about censorship issues."[4] *Publishers Weekly* found the book "very smart," its story "credible and entertaining," and *Booklist* described Lasky's arguments about intellectual freedom "convincing and disturbing."[5] Most critics agreed that Lasky had focused on crucial issues and made a strong statement about censorship. However, in some of the harshest responses to any of Lasky's YA fiction, some critics saw the novel as more sermon than story. The *New Advocate,* while noting that Lasky "captures the closed and single-minded nature of faces we often see on the news," also found that "Lasky lays it on a bit thick."[6] The most critical reviews objected mainly to the "one-dimensional" and "unconvincing" characterizations of the religious fundamentalists and to a plot they viewed as manipulated to suit Lasky's argument.[7] "[O]verprogrammed with contrivances," said the *Bulletin of the Center for Children's Books*.[8] Several reviewers found Gray and his model nonsexist family among the most objectionable contrivances, too good to be true.

One can argue that some of the criticism is unwarranted. *Memoirs* is, after all, Harper's story, told from her viewpoint; she is (like most first-person narrators of YA fiction) intended to be a reliable voice and is in no position to weigh the complexities of all the issues at stake. Nor is Lasky trying for a more sympathetic portrayal of the religious right. As a writer, she has been true to her own perspective. One review that unfavorably compared Lasky's novel to another about fundamentalists whose actions are "an abiding testament to their deep, abiding faith" missed the point entirely: Lasky was not writing any such testimonial.[9]

To the contrary. As *Kirkus Reviews* observed, Lasky's sympathies are "obvious."[10] Almost all the fundamentalists in this story are offensive on a grand scale, with the implication that religious fundamentalism and racial bigotry are all but synonymous. Has Lasky, then, given us an inaccurate portrait? Any answer, of course, depends on the reader's own perception of religious fundamentalists, but it should be noted that Lasky has gone to some length to balance her material. A letter from one of Harper's favorite authors makes clear that this novel is neither antireligious nor anti-Christian; furthermore, although Harper's father behaves in a heavy-handed manner and his reaction to Gammy's song seems extreme, Lasky has countered him with a more sympathetic portrayal of Harper's mother: she is a submissive wife whose newfound faith has indeed proven a salvation and who is trying to do her best by her family. As for the Reverend LePage, he seems an authentic portrayal—neither satiric nor overstated—of many "showbiz" televangelists who have frequented the cable networks. The worst of the fundamentalists—Weesie's friend Cindy and her domineering mother—are indeed so appalling that they are more caricature than characterization, and Gray is perhaps a shade too good, his appearance too facile, his family too perfect.

But the novel offsets these problems with some definite strengths, such as the quality of Lasky's writing and, in particular, Harper's characterization (one reader wrote that she was "like the sister I never had"[11]). It is more than a tract about censorship. "How will censors react to this book?" wondered Lesley Farmer in the *Book Report* (Farmer, 45). Lasky replies that she has heard nothing from them. With the exception of the librarian who objected to *Traces of Life,* none of Lasky's books has received attention from censors or would-be censors. However, *Memoirs* has led to several speaking engagements on the subject of censorship.

Memoirs is most often discussed in terms of its censorship theme, but Lasky insists that thought control, not censorship, was her main thematic subject (although the latter is, of course, one aspect of the former). She plays a variation on this theme in *Alice Rose and Sam,* her historical novel for middle-school readers that imagines a friendship between Alice Rose, a young girl living in Virginia City during the Civil War, and Sam Clemens, later known as Mark Twain.

Although the central tensions of the story derive from Alice Rose's grief over her mother's recent death and her unhappiness with life in the rough, dirty mining town, *Alice Rose and Sam,* like *Memoirs,* exposes the self-righteous posturing of Christian proselytizers as sham. One of the novel's villains, Jewel Petty, represents herself as a God-fearing Christian. From her lofty moral perch, she tries to impose her religion and moral judgments on Alice Rose and the rest of the town. She and her husband, a corrupt judge, are later revealed to be part of a racist band of Confederate thieves plotting to claim the major share of the rich Comstock Lode.

Sam Clemens' comments on religion, all drawn from his published essays, his notebooks, and his novels, are both scathing and humorous, leaving little doubt of Lasky's—and the implied reader's—skepticism toward fundamentalist Christianity. For example, Sam tells Alice Rose, "To know God is to know nature. I knew a river once and that is as close as I ever came to knowing God" (*ARS,* 86). His comments amaze and puzzle Alice Rose. "Then you don't have to be a Christian?" she asks. To which Sam replies, "I would say it helps not to be. There has only been one true Christian in the entire history of the earth, Jesus Christ, and they caught and crucified him early.... Furthermore, it is my considered opinion that if Jesus Christ came back to earth right now, there is one thing that he would not be.... A Christian" (87–88).

Sam's views on the Bible are equally unorthodox. "You can cite the Bible and get anything approved," he says, comparing the Good Book to a drugstore where various religious sects can choose a remedy from its contents to assuage their particular metaphysical headaches. He also claims that although the Bible contains some good morals, it also has "upwards of a thousand lies" (*ARS*, 84). When Alice Rose presses him to name just one, Sam paraphrases a passage in Deuteronomy that forbids

> " 'daughters [to] use divination [and] hocus-pocus stuff ... for all those things are an abomination unto the Lord and that because they are the Lord thy God doth drive them out from before thee.' " Now the Bible said 'drive.' I would think just picking those so-called witches up in a stagecoach and depositing them somewhere else would suffice, but no, not for some rabid Bible-toting Christian. They got to burn these charmers! ... Then, lo and behold, it was discovered that there was no such thing as witches and never has been." (85)

Sam's speech points directly to the subject of Lasky's novel *Beyond the Burning Time*. While ostensibly about the Salem witchcraft trials, it, like *Memoirs*, takes as its main concern the issue of thought control by religious zealots. After she finished *Beyond the Burning Time*, she saw that this novel and *Memoirs* shared corresponding themes. "I realized I had written the same book twice," Lasky says with rueful humor. Perhaps, but she tells two very different stories.

Beyond the Burning Time

In *Beyond the Burning Time*, Lasky moves back to 1691, three hundred years prior to Harper's story and two hundred years earlier than the nineteenth century of her other historical fiction. The novel recounts an infamous chapter of American history, the shameful story of the Salem witchcraft trials. However, Lasky goes beyond the familiar tale of hysterical young women accusing innocent people of witchcraft: she also explores the personal, political, and economic factors that complicated the situation.

Lasky had long been intrigued by this period and discomfited by the transformation of Salem, the site of such tragedy, into a popular tourist attraction. Always interested in adolescents' personal viewpoints on historical events, she tried to imagine the perspective of a young adult who lived through that time. Then one day she found herself imagining what it would have been like for someone whose mother was charged with witchcraft and condemned to die. Thus Mary Chase, the novel's 12-year-old protagonist, was born.

Mary and her mother, Virginia, live alone, on the family's farm in Salem Village, Massachusetts. Mary's father has died two years earlier, and her brother Caleb lives several miles away, in the port of Salem Town, where he works as an apprentice at a shipyard. The opening chapter quickly establishes the basic circumstances of the story. The reader learns that the slave Tituba has practiced "little sorceries" for a group of young women from Salem Village, predicting whom they might marry. All of them are now afflicted with "fits." In economical and vivid language, Lasky evokes the bitter January weather, suggests the superstitious mind-set of the times that fostered the hysteria, and introduces Mary as a practical individual who is more concerned about the future of her family's barley crop than the identity of a husband.

Mary exemplifies Lasky's "keyhole" approach to historical fiction, enabling the reader to see the story from what Lasky describes as "the perspective of ordinary people during extraordinary times" ("Keyhole," 6). She is a completely fictional character, but like Thad and Julian of *The Bone Wars* her life intersects with historic personages: the "afflicted" girls and their victims, Cotton Mather and his coterie of Puritan ministers and judges, the governor of Massachusetts. Lasky explains the mix of fiction and historical fact in an author's note: "While I have altered facts in this novel, I have tried to remain faithful to the historical period in which they occurred."[12]

Indeed, the novel conveys a wealth of detail about the period and the place: the physical hardships of life, farming and shipbuilding practices, family customs and social mores, religious beliefs and medical procedures. However, the main historical interest lies in the witchcraft trials, and Lasky's telling of the events leading to them reflects her meticulous research. She made ample use of scholarly work on the period and of documents in the Salem archives, even taking some dialogue directly from these records. Her efforts serve to invest the story of Mary and her family with credible urgency.

Although Mary's family subscribes to Puritan beliefs, they are not swept up in what Mary thinks of as the "strangeness." Virginia is a strong woman, judicious and charitable, and her deity is a God of hope and gladness. In Virginia's home, there is "no room for dread" (*BBT*, 17). But her unorthodox behavior foreshadows ill fortune. Virginia has taught her daughter to read, contrary to accepted practices; in 1691, reading was an endeavor reserved for men and was "most unusual for women, let alone girls" (14). And Virginia is quick to disparage the accusations of witchcraft as "nonsense," even as a friend warns her not to say another word.

Lasky makes clear that this reluctance to speak out, the rigid thought control exacted by the zealous Puritan theocracy, is exactly the element necessary to promote the hysteria. Well-meaning villagers who also recognize the girls' fits as "nonsense" fear talking freely outside their homes. Mary grasps that minding one's tongue can lead to minding one's thoughts, but she, too, is cowed into silence. Even Mary's brother Caleb, briefly visiting the village, is careful to guard his own speech, for the entire place seems "tainted," and he doubts that there is anyone in Salem Village "with whom one could talk sense" (*BBT*, 142). The girls' visions "seemed to have a powerful contagion" (157), for the silence feeds the hysteria, precluding any chance of balancing it with outspoken common sense. The result is what Lasky describes as a "topsy-turvy" effect: the villagers perpetrate the very evil that they so fear, much as the zealotry in *Memoirs of a Bookbat* generates not Christian love but suspicion and hatred. The description of what ensues makes a powerful point about the dangers of witch hunts both literal and figurative:

> The witch within became the witch outside, and the people could not resist pointing their fingers and crying out. Their souls had become addicted to destroying, and they were more intent and obsessed with this destruction than the angel thrown from heaven, Lucifer himself. (232)

As the hysterical girls indict more and more victims, among them the most pious and righteous in the village, Mary's sense of apprehension grows. Finally, her own mother is decried as a witch and hauled off to prison. The remaining chapters trace the suspenseful events leading to Mary and Caleb's rescue of Virginia. An epilogue follows Mary into her 99th year; she is reading a diary entry by Virginia's second husband, a sea captain instrumental in her rescue. His diary sketches the circumstances of her mother's later years, an example of the mimetic fiction that appears so frequently in Lasky's work. Mary's reflections provide a brief synopsis of her adult life. She is the matriarch of a large family and, with Caleb, cofounder of a successful shipyard. In the closing sentence, Mary begins to write of her experiences during the witchcraft trials with the same resolute spirit that sustained her through them. In those terrible months, she evolved from docile child to rebellious hero, acquiring courage and determination. Her development is twofold: she grows more independent in thought and action, and she revises her ideas about the spiritual realm.

Initially, Mary has a trustful and obedient nature. Although no stranger to hardships—her father has died a sudden death, and the family's crops are subject to the whims of nature—she feels some degree of security in a world that promises just rewards for virtuous behavior, and she willingly abides by its rules. The only hint in the early chapters that Mary's soul harbors the "guerrilla" or rebel common to Lasky's YA protagonists is her longing to transcend the constraints imposed by her gender. "Ah, to be a boy!" she thinks (*BBT*, 5), contemplating her brother's opportunities at the shipyard. She, too, would like to use her hands to create marvelous things from wood. "She envied her brother.... She would rather be a master carpenter than a king" (17–18). And she is learning the stars, an interest other Lasky characters share that signals, always, a lofty perspective.

Mary tries (although unsuccessfully) to pray away the envy, never thinking to question the established order. But as the hysteria spreads throughout the village and the dread laps closer and closer to her own door, she begins to shed her compliant self. When her mother is arrested, outraged bitterness replaces Mary's customary submission, and she feels as if "she could have plunged a knife" into the heart of one villager who partakes in her mother's humiliation (*BBT,* 176). She comes to feel most comfortable "in the half light and the darkness" (241). After Virginia is sentenced to death by hanging, Mary discovers within her soul "another nature capable of deception and violence.... Within this soul, she imagined both a moon and a sun; and she knew that a strange eclipse had begun to occur" (241). She now understands the duality of the human heart, its potential for both purity and iniquity, hope and despair. Only after her mother's rescue appears imminent does she feel "the darkness inside begin to lighten, and the sun within her [begin] to slide past the moon" (250). Significantly, this occurs when Mary takes control of her fate. Like Harper, she has learned that she must think and act according to her convictions, that to accede to the powerful dictates of any community can be riskier than defying them. The path less traveled may be the safest course.

The figurative eclipse of Mary's soul finds a parallel in the weather of Salem Village. As Mary scurries home in the opening scene, the winter light is "hard and metallic.... It would be dark soon" (*BBT,* 1). The winter darkness that descends is an apt metaphor for the spiritual darkness that follows. When the sun does shine in a later scene, Mary is suspicious of it, knowing that spring is still a long way off and that this is "not the time of birth, or renewal," that it is "still a dying time in a long winter yet to come" (48). Appropriately, Virginia's rescue occurs at dawn and coincides with the spring thaw.

Mary's personal transformation corresponds to her evolving concept of God. Just as at the outset she accepts the limitations of her female role as rightly preordained, so she accepts without question the Puritan theology that conceives God as locked with Satan in a literal battle for human souls. When she hears her mother's friend Rebecca Nurse describe the girls' fits, she imagines—despite Rebecca's reasonable explanation that the girls "are coming into their spring" and "want attention"—hideous scenes of the afflicted girls wrestling with the invisible world of evil, each so vivid that she is convinced of their veracity: "Was it not real in some way? How could it not be?" (*BBT,* 31–34). And when one of the girls begins an "antic dance" during a church service, as if she had been attacked by a "fiend . . . with hot claws," Mary believes that she can "see long, angry marks scraping across young Ann's neck" (59).

As events spiral out of control, her belief is shaken. Even as she admires the work of a "clever God" responsible for the marvels of the natural world, she wonders about God's hand in creating the people responsible for the hysteria. Her conjectures frighten her: "She had never questioned God in this way" (*BBT*, 125). Later, concealed in a closet and watching as Virginia is stripped and searched for signs of witchcraft, she doubts the very existence of a benevolent deity. "There was no God in such a world. . . . Satan had won, and he was on his knees, peering under the skirts, examining the thighs of her mother" (179).

Upon her brother's insistence, Mary leaves Salem Village and hides in Salem Town but returns surreptitiously to her home following her mother's arrest. The house is empty, its contents confiscated by officers of the court, but Mary finds in her old room a beautifully crafted wooden box her brother made for her months earlier. Inside the box are lupine seeds, which she takes as a sign of hope and renewal, much as Meribah is affirmed by the seeds her father bequeaths to her in *Beyond the Divide*. Mary's religious faith stirs again, and she determines to trust "in a God who makes hope possible and faith not a dream" (*BBT*, 185). Mary has come full circle, from belief to doubt to belief, one that is stronger and healthier.

The structure of this novel is also circular. It begins in January and ends in January, 87 years later. In the closing lines, Mary remembers "the sun and the moon that she had imagined within her own soul that winter, and the strange eclipse that was about to begin" (*BBT*, 265). Then she takes up her pen to write the story of the "strangeness" that has just been told.

Writing in the third person, Lasky uses Mary's perspective as the principal lens through which the reader sees the story; although a peer of the afflicted girls, she is geographically and emotionally distanced from them. Thus her more objective viewpoint provides a moral yardstick by which to measure the other characters and events. She also serves to convey factual information about actual historical events not immediately relevant to her own story, as when, visiting Caleb, she brings news of recent developments in Salem Village. These summaries allow Lasky to work in details not easily handled otherwise.

Other facts are brought forward through frequent shifts in the narrative point of view. The broad swath of Lasky's historical fiction typically sweeps many characters into its path, and she often renders her story from a range of viewpoints. In *Beyond the Burning Time,* the reader is privy at one time or another to the perceptions not only of the many fictional characters—Virginia, her two children, and hired man Gilly—but of the historical figures as well: villagers, ministers, and politicians. An omniscient narrator also provides commentary on the partisan politics of the times.

In exploring the complex motives that culminated in the witchcraft trials, Lasky has included some material that is frankly sexual. Each of these scenes involves the attraction of a servant to an employer, perhaps signifying the seductive allure of power. The servant girl Mary Warren, whose relationship with John Proctor is historically documented, remembers with pleasure the first time she caught John looking at her breasts. When she lies awake at night, she sometimes hears the "rhythmic creaks" from his bedroom. Old enough to know what those sounds imply, she is pleased that the bedsprings have been silent "for many months now" (*BBT,* 150).[13]

Virginia arouses similar passions in Gilly, her retarded hired man, but unlike John Proctor, who appears cognizant of Mary Warren's feelings, she is oblivious to Gilly's emotions. His attraction begins when he steals a pair of Virginia's drawers that have blown from a clothesline and is stirred by thoughts of what the garment covers. He spies on her at night as she undresses, harboring images of Virginia's "tapering legs that glowed" and "the soft shadows of her thighs" (*BBT,* 85, 111). Although Gilly, unlike Mary Warren, is a fictitious character, their stories run parallel, and they both play significant roles in convicting their employers.

Contemporary representations of the Salem witchcraft trials often emphasize the adolescent sexual tensions that sparked the hysteria, but Lasky makes clear that it was the adults who fanned the early blaze into a full-fledged conflagration. Many factors fed the inferno: a feud between two of the richest families in the area; the lack of a governing charter that exposed the Commonwealth of Massachusetts to lawless forces; tensions between the inland, provincial Salem Village and the prosperous, coastal Salem Town; the self-aggrandizing motives of some of the ministers and judges; and the hunger—even lust—for spectacle that relieved life in Salem Village of its dreariness. Virginia accurately identifies the deadly mix of motives as she faces the constables and sheriff who have come to arrest her: "[Y]ou have become the Devil's instrument, and the Devil is not from the invisible world but from the visible—the world of money and land and failed businesses and disastrous enterprises" (*BBT*, 169–70). Lasky echoes Virginia's accusation in her author's note, stating that "old grudges, jealousy, and money had as much to do with the tragedy of Salem as superstitions" (270). Indeed, Lasky demonstrates that greed was not only a cause of the "contagion" but a result of it as well. The constables and sheriff responsible for confiscating property of the accused often kept some choice objects for themselves.

The vivid images typical of Lasky's fiction serve well to establish the story's bleak and frigid setting in a winter "cold enough to make things break" (*BBT*, 22). But Lasky saves her most incisive images to distinguish among the large cast of characters. Goody Dawson, a gossipmongering busybody, has a face like a "potato: smooth and slightly yellowish with a few darker pinpoint-sized speckles. Her mouth was very tiny and a bit lost, tucked between her rounded cheeks and chin" (9). Rebecca Nurse and her sister, who dares to label the girls' fits as a "travesty," sail from the meetinghouse "like sprightly ships in a smart breeze" (59).

Beyond the Burning Time has drawn critical praise from many quarters and earned several awards: American Library Association's Best Book for Young Adults, New York Public Library's 100 Best Books of the Year, and the Sequoyah Young Adult Book Award. Reviewers admired the scope and depth of Lasky's research. Carolyn Noah echoed the response of many critics when she described the novel as "well researched and documented with extensive notes" and recommended it as a "readable, engrossing, and sometimes exciting tale."[14] *Kirkus Reviews* found the book "appealing" and "rich in details about life in Puritan New England," and the *Horn Book* admired the "frightening immediacy" of the story.[15] However, several critics expressed reservations about the sheer accumulation of information that, as one noted, swamped the story. *Publishers Weekly* was perhaps the harshest critic. Its review described the novel as an "overblown narrative," a "soap opera with shoe buckles."[16]

Hazel Rochman voiced reservations about the "huge cast of characters" and the "abrupt switches in point of view," qualities characteristic of Lasky's historical fiction. However, Rochman also articulated what may be the fairest assessment of this novel in her closing statement: "Lasky's research is meticulous: she draws on court records and contemporary accounts to show the community madness. The history overwhelms the fiction, but both are compelling."[17]

Conclusion

Both *Memoirs of a Bookbat* and *Beyond the Burning Time* testify to the value that Lasky places on freedom of thought and expression, and letters from her readers confirm that the issues she raises strike responsive chords. A managing editor of a publishing house other than Lasky's was so moved after reading these novels that she "felt compelled" to write Lasky to say how "touching" she found them.[18] Together, *Memoirs* and *Burning Time* deliver an unswerving message: the religious fundamentalists who would take no prisoners are themselves imprisoned by their own hunger for power and by their narrow-minded suspicion of the "other" that is as contagious as influenza. The Puritans drive themselves to certain doom; the fate of the contemporary religious right has yet to be sealed. But as Lasky shows, the price of thought control is high for those who attempt to enforce it: hatred, greed, deceit, rebellion. Almost four hundred years after Shakespeare lived, Lasky echoes in these two novels a sentiment from the bard's *Winter's Tale:* "It is an heretic that makes the fire / Not she which burns in't."[19]

Kathy at a book signing
Courtesy Kathryn Lasky

The Knight family: Max, Kathy, Chris, and Meribah, November 1997
Elsa Dorfman

7. Searching for Kathryn Lasky: Epilogue

Many of Kathryn Lasky's young adult novels end with epilogues that provide brief glimpses into her characters' future lives. Rachel of *The Night Journey* goes off to college, Thad and Julian of *The Bone Wars* settle into old age as men successful in both their professional and personal lives, Sarah of *Pageant* joins the Peace Corps, Mary of *Beyond the Burning Time* lives into her 99th year to write about the Salem witchcraft trials, Lucy and Afrika of *True North* are reunited decades later. These epilogues are tidy: they gather up loose ends and close with finality.

It seems appropriate to conclude a search for Kathryn Lasky Knight with this same finality, but of course such an ending works only in fiction. An epilogue for an author who is still very much alive and hard at work must take a different route, looking back in order to look forward, settling for probability rather than prediction. Even Lasky's own imagination, which has given life to so many stories, balks at creating future scenarios for herself. "I'll keep writing," she says. Beyond that, she has no definitive answer: "Who knows?" Still, a reader in search of Kathryn Lasky Knight can guess what to expect of her in the coming years, for in the accumulated pages of her work is a clear picture of this writer who wakes each morning to "reinvent the world."

Her unfailing curiosity will lead her to more photo essays about the natural world and the people who study it. She will write more stories that illustrate, like her own life, the warmth of old friendships and the lure of new places, the human need for both community and autonomy. Because her imagination is sparked by the paradoxes and moral dilemmas stamped upon our history, she will still be sniffing out the rats, still finding in a world turned topsy turvy by greed and cruelty and ignorance the promise of hope. She will continue to peer through the keyhole at scenes from the past, coming upon characters who empower themselves by working to empower others.

Like most writers, she resists talking about ideas for books she has yet to write, but they are there—in her head and in her file boxes. More children's nonfiction and fiction. More young adult novels. More biographies and adult fiction. More stories set in the here and now. More stories that reach back into the past. And always, whatever the genre or audience, all kinds of people in all kinds of places. And in their complicated humanity, an unblinking recognition of their all-too-human failings and a hymn to their human virtues, to wit and empathy and intelligence and courage. To courage, perhaps, most of all.

Notes and References

1. Searching for Kathryn Lasky: The Early Years

1. Kathryn Lasky, telephone interview by author, 27 August 1997. All quotes by Lasky not otherwise attributed in the text are drawn from this and other interviews, including another telephone interview, 10 June 1996, and personal interviews on 23 November 1996 in Chicago and on 3 October 1997 in Cambridge, Massachusetts.

2. Most of the information about Hortense and Marven Lasky is drawn from the early chapters of Kathryn Lasky's *Atlantic Circle* (New York: W. W. Norton, 1985); hereafter cited in text as *AC*.

3. *Speaking for Ourselves,* ed. Don Gallo (Urbana, Illinois: NCTE, 1990), 114.

4. Susan Reicha, "Kathryn Lasky," in *Something about the Author,* ed. Donna Olendorf, vol. 69 (Detroit: Gale Research, 1992), 131.

5. Quoted by Barbara G. Samuels, "Kathryn Lasky," in *Writers for Young Adults,* ed. Ted Hipple, vol. 2 (New York: Charles Scribner's Sons, 1997), 207.

6. Christopher Knight, interview by author, 3 October 1997, Cambridge; all unattributed quotations by Christopher Knight are drawn from this interview.

7. Kathryn Lasky, *Tugboats Never Sleep* (New York: Little, Brown, 1977), unpaged.

8. Susan Ebershoff-Coles, *Library Journal* (December 1984): 2278.

9. Christopher Buckley, *New York Times Book Review* (10 February 1985): 15.

10. Kathryn Lasky, "Keyhole History," SIGNAL (Spring 1997): 9. This article was adapted from a speech Lasky gave at the National Council of Teachers of English, Chicago, November 1996; hereafter cited in text as "Keyhole."

11. Kathryn Lasky, "Reflections on Nonfiction," *Horn Book Magazine* (September/October 1985): 531; hereafter cited in text as "Reflections."

12. Denise Perry Donavin, "The *Booklist* Interview," ALA *Booklist* (1 October 1991): 246; hereafter cited in text as Donavin.

2. Searching for Kathryn Lasky: The Writer

1. Kathryn Lasky, *Mumbo Jumbo* (New York: Pocket Books, 1990), 3.
2. Jane F. Cullinane, *School Library Journal* (May 1983): 73.
3. Betsy Hearne, *Bulletin of the Center for Children's Books* (March 1992): 184.
4. Meredith Charpentier, telephone interview by author, 14 November 1997. All other quotations from Charpentier are drawn from this interview.
5. Ellen Mandel, *Booklist* (1 May 1990): 1707.
6. Jon R. Luoma, *New York Times Book Review* (24 June 1990): 29.
7. Betsy Hearne, *Bulletin of the Center for Children's Books* (June 1990): 245.
8. Cathryn A. Camper, *School Library Journal* (June 1990): 132.
9. Kathryn Lasky, *Dinosaur Dig* (New York: Morrow, 1990), unpaged.
10. Cathryn A. Camper, *School Library Journal* (May 1990): 98.
11. Malcolm W. Browne, *New York Times Book Review* (24 June 1990): 28.
12. Stephanie Zvirin, *Booklist* (1 June 1993): 805.
13. Roger Sutton, *Bulletin of the Center for Children's Books* (February 1993): 181.
14. Ellen Fader, *School Library Journal* (April 1992): 138.
15. Margaret A. Bush, *Horn Book* (November/December 1993): 755.
16. Susan Oliver, *School Library Journal* (September 1993): 244.
17. Jessie Meudell, *School Library Journal* (October 1994): 135, and Roger Sutton, *Bulletin of the Center for Children's Books* (October 1994): 54.
18. Carolyn Phelan, *Booklist* (1 April 1997): 1330.
19. Kathryn Lasky, *The Most Beautiful Roof in the World: Exploring the Rainforest Canopy* (New York: Harcourt, Brace, 1997), unpaged.
20. Denise Perry Donavin, *Booklist* (15 May 1986): 1360.
21. Kathleen Maio, *Wilson Library Bulletin* (December 1986): 53; *Publishers Weekly* (18 April 1986): 51.
22. Denise Perry Donavin, *Booklist* (1 June 1994): 1777.
23. Pam Spencer, *School Library Journal* (March 1995): 235; *Publishers Weekly* (27 June 1994): 59.
24. Kathryn Lasky, *Dark Swan* (New York: St. Martin's, 1994), 11.
25. Kathryn Lasky, *Double Trouble Squared* (New York: Harcourt Brace Jovanovich, 1991), 224.

26. Kathryn Lasky, "Creativity in a Boom Industry," *Horn Book* (November/December 1991): 707; hereafter cited as "Creativity."
27. *Publishers Weekly* (2 November 1992): 72.
28. Julie Halverstadt, *School Library Journal* (December 1993): 114.
29. Kathryn Lasky, *Alice Rose and Sam* (New York: Hyperion, 1998), 249; hereafter cited as *ARS*.
30. Kathryn Lasky, *She's Wearing a Dead Bird on Her Head* (New York: (Hyperion, 1995), unpaged.
31. Joanne Schott, *Quill Quire* (November 1995): 47.
32. Kathryn Lasky, *The Librarian Who Measured the Earth* (New York: Little, Brown, 1994), unpaged.
33. Joanne Schott, *Quill Quire* (October 1994): 50.
34. Steven Engelfried, *School Library Journal* (September 1994): 209.
35. Kathryn Lasky, "To Stingo with Love," *New Advocate* (Winter 1996): 5.
36. Violet J. Harris, "Continuing Dilemmas, Debates, and Delights in Multicultural Literature," *New Advocate* (Spring 1996): 114.
37. Kathryn Lasky, letter to the editor, *New Advocate* (Summer 1996): viii.
38. Anne Leit, telephone interview by author, 12 November 1997.

3. Toads in the Garden: Kathryn Lasky's Approach to Historical Fiction

1. Thomas Mallon, "Writing Historical Fiction," *The American Scholar* (Autumn 1992): 604.
2. Joan I. Glazer and Burney Williams III, *Introduction to Children's Literature* (New York: McGraw-Hill, 1979), 360; hereafter cited in text as Glazer and Williams.
3. Arthea J.S. Reed, *Reaching Adolescents: The Young Adult Book and the School* (New York: Macmillan, 1994), 121.
4. Joan Blos, " 'I Catherine Cabot Hall': The Journal as Historical Fiction," in *The Voice of the Narrator in Children's Literature: Insights from Writers and Critics,* ed. Charlotte F. Otten and Gary D. Schmidt (New York: Greenwood Press, 1989), 278; hereafter cited in text as Blos.
5. Kathryn Lasky, *A Journey to the New World: The Diary of Remember Patience Whipple* (New York: Scholastic, 1996), 28; hereafter cited in text as *Journey*.
6. Kathryn Lasky, *Dreams in the Golden Country: The Diary of Ziporrah Feldman, a Jewish Immigrant Girl* (New York: Scholastic, 1998), 4; hereafter cited in text as *Dreams*.
7. Susan Pine, *School Library Journal* (August 1996): 144.
8. Lynne B. Hawkins, *Voice of Youth Advocates (VOYA)* (October 1996): 210.

9. Ann Schlee, "Only a Lampholder: On Writing Historical Fiction," in *Innocence and Experience,* ed. Barbara Harrison and Gregory Maguire (New York: Lothrop, Lee, & Shepard, 1987), 265.

10. Henry Seidel Canby, as quoted by Kenneth I. Donelson and Alleen Pace Nilsen, *Literature for Today's Young Adult,* 3d ed. (Glenview, Ill.: Scott, Foresman, 1989), 169; book hereafter cited in text as Donelson and Nilsen.

11. Jill Paton Walsh, "History Is Fiction," *Horn Book* (February 1972): 23.

12. Kathryn Lasky, "The Fiction of History: Or, What Did Miss Kitty Nearly Do?" *New Advocate* (Summer 1990): 165; hereafter cited in text as "Kitty."

13. Meredith Charpentier to Kathryn Lasky, 9 December 1980.

14. Kathryn Lasky, *The Night Journey* (New York: Puffin Books, 1986), unpaged; hereafter cited in text as *NJ.* Ann Lasky Smith was musically talented. A contemporary of Irving Berlin, she wrote and published songs for Tin Pan Alley.

15. Lasky recounts a similar anecdote about her own ancestors in *Atlantic Circle,* 28.

16. Peter Kennerley, *School Librarian* (June 1983): 144.

17. *Bulletin of the Center for Children's Books* (December 1981): 72.

18. Ilene Cooper, *Booklist* (15 November 1981): 439.

19. Some of Lasky's ancestors actually immigrated from Nikolayev.

20. Ethel L. Heins, *Horn Book* (April 1982): 166.

4. Smelling the Rat:
Journeys into the Nineteenth Century

1. The problem stemmed from an editor who, dissatisfied with Lasky's first chapter, requested repeated revisions aimed at getting the plot under way more quickly. Finally, an editor at another publishing house encouraged Lasky to finish her story, recognizing that she needed the freedom to explore her story before taking it through extensive revisions.

2. Kathryn Lasky, *Beyond the Divide* (New York: Macmillan, 1983), 5; hereafter cited in text as *BD.*

3. Lasky gleefully confesses to writing these awful verses—adept parodies of the maudlin poetry in vogue at the time—herself.

4. Although the term "Native American" has mostly replaced the earlier, less accurate, and sometimes demeaning "Indian," both *Beyond the Divide* and *The Bone Wars* use the latter term, which is entirely appropriate to each novel's historical setting. The discussion of these novels reflects that usage.

5. Natalie Babbitt, *New York Times Book Review* (21 August 1983): 26.

6. *Bulletin of the Center for Children's Books* (June 1983): 192.
7. Dorothy Lettus, *VOYA* (October 1983): 204.
8. In an author's note at the end of *The Bone Wars,* Lasky writes that she based the characters of the Harvard and Yale paleontologists on actual professors from those universities known for their "ungentlemanly" and "sleazy" behavior. The character of DeMott is based on an arrogant English scientist who invented the word *dinosaur.*
9. Kathryn Lasky, *The Bone Wars* (New York: William Morrow, 1988), 48; hereafter cited in text as *BW.*
10. Yvonne A. Frey, *School Library Journal* (November 1988): 126.
11. Susan Terris, *New York Times Book Review* (18 December 1988): 30.
12. *Publishers Weekly* (25 November 1988): 67.
13. Zena Sutherland, *Bulletin of the Center for Children's Books* (November 1988): 77.
14. Kathryn Lasky, *True North: A Novel of the Underground Railroad* (New York: Blue Sky Press, 1996), 259–60; hereafter cited in text as *TN.*
15. Lucy Bradford is an entirely fictitious character. However, her ancestor William Bradford is a historically significant personage, the architect of the Mayflower Compact (*TN,* 263).
16. Lasky has borrowed the name Levi from her husband's family tree. Levi Knight was renowned for his laziness and remembered as a grouch, but Lasky believes that he was "probably a folk hero before such types were appreciated" (*AC,* 19).
17. *Kirkus Reviews* (1 October 1996): 1470.
18. Carol Schene, *School Library Journal* (December 1996): 139.
19. Karen Simonetti, *Booklist* (15 November 1996): 579.
20. *Publishers Weekly* (15 July 1996): 75.

5. Contemporary Lives: Family and Friends

1. Kathryn Lasky, *Prank* (New York: Macmillan, 1984), 18; hereafter cited in text.
2. Hannah Arendt, *Eichmann in Jerusalem: A Report on the Banality of Evil* (New York: Viking, 1963).
3. Judith Mitchell, *VOYA* (February 1985): 328.
4. Pat Harrington, *School Library Journal* (October 1984): 168.
5. Albert V. Schwartz, *Interracial Books for Children Bulletin* (1 November 1985): 7.
6. Kathryn Lasky, *Home Free* (New York: Macmillan, 1985), 114; hereafter cited in text as *HF.*
7. Ilene Cooper, *Booklist* (15 January 1986): 758–59.
8. *Bulletin of the Center for Children's Books* (February 1986): 112.

9. Sara Miller, *School Library Journal* (March 1986): 176.
10. Marijo Duncan, *VOYA* (October 1986): 145.
11. Kathryn Lasky, *Pageant* (New York: Four Winds Press, 1986), 5; hereafter cited in text.
12. Lasky also alludes to her experience as a shepherd in *The Night Journey*. At one point, Rachel is hunting for some material for a costume when she discovers a musty shepherd's robe stored in the basement of her home. Her mother explains that she wore it in a school Christmas pageant.
13. Meredith Charpentier to Kathryn Lasky, 4 February 1985.
14. Hazel Rochman, *Beyond Borders* (Chicago: American Library Association, 1993), 201; Alba Quinones Endicott, *English Journal* (April 1992): 42–43.
15. Denise M. Wilms, *Booklist* (November 15, 1986): 507.
16. Kathryn Lasky, *The Widow of Oz* (New York: W. W. Norton, 1989), 46; hereafter cited in text as *WO*.
17. *Publishers Weekly* (21 April 1989): 81; Denise Perry Donavin, *Booklist* (1 June 1989): 169.

6. Danger: Zealots at Work

1. Kathryn Lasky, *Memoirs of a Bookbat* (New York: Harcourt Brace, 1994), 31; hereafter cited in text as *MB*.
2. After *Memoirs* was published, Lasky learned that gerbils have been illegal in California for many years because of the danger of their getting loose and wiping out native species. Although Lasky did extensive research for this novel on the activities of fundamentalist groups, the information about gerbils escaped her; otherwise, she could have substituted hamsters, which are legal.
3. Lesley Farmer, *Book Report* (November 94): 45; hereafter cited in text as Farmer.
4. *Horn Book Guide* (Fall 1994): 321; Kathleen Crawford et al., "Exploring the World through Multiple Literacies," *The Reading Teacher* (April 1995): 600.
5. *Publishers Weekly* (23 May 1994): 90; Hazel Rochman, *Booklist* (15 April 1994): 1526.
6. Mary Jane Blasi, *New Advocate* (Fall 1994): 296–97.
7. Alice Casey Smith, *School Library Journal* (July 1994): 119.
8. Roger Sutton, *Bulletin of the Center for Children's Books* (April 1994): 264.
9. Alice Casey Smith, *School Library Journal* (July 1994): 119.
10. *Kirkus Reviews* (1 June 1994): 776.
11. Sarah Popiel to Kathryn Lasky, 3 March 1995.

12. Kathryn Lasky, *Beyond the Burning Time* (New York: Blue Sky Press, 1994), 267; hereafter cited in text as *BBT*.
13. Arthur Miller used the relationship between John Proctor and his servant girl as the main plot line for his play *The Crucible*.
14. Carolyn Noah, *School Library Journal* (January 1995): 108.
15. *Kirkus Reviews* (15 October 1994): 1410; Mary M. Burns, *Horn Book* (March 1995): 200.
16. *Publishers Weekly* (17 October 1994): 82.
17. Hazel Rochman, *Booklist* (15 October 1994): 420.
18. Cindi Di Marzo to Kathryn Lasky, 10 January 1995.
19. William Shakespeare, *The Winter's Tale,* 2.3.116.

Selected Bibliography

Primary Works

Young Adult Novels

The Night Journey. New York: Warne, 1981. (National Jewish Book Award for Children, ALA Notable Book)
Beyond the Divide. New York: Macmillan, 1983. (ALA Best Book, *New York Times* Notable Book)
Prank. New York: Macmillan, 1984. (ALA Best Book)
Home Free. New York: Macmillan, 1985.
Pageant. New York: Four Winds Press, 1986. (ALA Notable Book)
The Bone Wars. New York: Morrow, 1988.
Beyond the Burning Time. New York: Scholastic, 1994.
Memoirs of a Bookbat. New York: Harcourt Brace, 1994.
True North: A Novel of the Underground Railroad. New York: Blue Sky Press, 1996.

Fiction for Younger Readers

I Have Four Names for My Grandfather. New York: Little, Brown, 1976.
My Island Grandmother. New York: Warne, 1979.
Jem's Island. New York: Charles Scribner's Sons, 1982.
Sea Swan. New York: Macmillan, 1988.
Double Trouble Squared. New York: Harcourt Brace Jovanovich, 1991.
Fourth of July Bear. New York: Morrow, 1991.
I Have an Aunt on Marlborough Street. New York: Macmillan, 1992.
Shadows in the Water. New York: Harcourt Brace, 1992.
The Tantrum. New York: Macmillan, 1993.
A Voice in the Wind. New York: Harcourt Brace, 1993.
Cloud Eyes. New York: Harcourt Brace, 1994.
The Solo. New York: Macmillan, 1994.
The Gates of the Wind. New York: Harcourt Brace, 1995.
Pond Year. New York: Candlewick, 1995.
She's Wearing a Dead Bird on Her Head. New York: Hyperion, 1995.

A Journey to the New World: The Diary of Remember Patience Whipple. New York: Scholastic, 1996.
Lunch Bunnies. New York: Harcourt Brace, 1996.
Hercules: The Man, the Myth, the Hero. New York: Hyperion, 1997.
Marven of the Great North Woods. New York: Harcourt Brace, 1997. (National Jewish Book Award for Children)
Alice Rose and Sam. New York: Hyperion, 1998.

Nonfiction for Younger Readers

Agatha's Alphabet. New York: Rand McNally, 1975.
Tugboats Never Sleep. New York: Little, Brown, 1977.
Tall Ships. New York: Charles Scribner's Sons, 1978.
Dollmaker: The Eyelight and the Shadow. New York: Charles Scribner's Sons, 1981.
The Weaver's Gift. New York: Warne, 1981. (Boston Globe–Horn Book Award for Nonfiction, ALA Notable Book)
Sugaring Time. New York: Macmillan, 1983. (Newbery Honor Book, ALA Notable Book)
A Baby for Max. New York: Charles Scribner's Sons, 1984.
Puppeteer. New York: Macmillan, 1985. (ALA Notable Book)
Traces of Life: The Origins of Humankind. New York: Morrow, 1989.
Dinosaur Dig. New York: Morrow, 1990.
Surtsey: The Newest Place on Earth. New York: Hyperion, 1992. (ALA Notable Book)
Think Like an Eagle: At Work with a Wildlife Photographer. New York: Little, Brown, 1992.
Monarchs. New York: Harcourt Brace, 1993. (Parents' Choice Silver Medal)
Searching for Laura Ingalls: A Reader's Journey. New York: Macmillan, 1993.
Days of the Dead. New York: Hyperion, 1994.
The Librarian Who Measured the Earth. New York: Little, Brown, 1994.
The Most Beautiful Roof in the World: Exploring the Rainforest Canopy. New York: Harcourt Brace, 1997.
A Brilliant Streak: The Making of Mark Twain. New York: Harcourt Brace, 1998.
Shadows in the Dawn: The Lemurs of Madagascar. New York: Harcourt Brace, 1998.

Adult Fiction and Nonfiction (published under Kathryn Lasky Knight)

Atlantic Circle. New York: Norton, 1985.
Trace Elements. New York: Norton, 1986.

The Widow of Oz. New York: Norton, 1989.
Mortal Words. New York: Simon & Schuster, 1990.
Mumbo Jumbo. New York: Simon & Schuster, 1991.
Dark Swan. New York: St. Martin's, 1994.

Articles

"The Fiction of History: Or, What Did Miss Kitty Really Do?" *New Advocate* 3 (Summer 1990): 157–166.
"Creativity in a Boom Industry." *Horn Book Magazine* (November/December 1991): 705–11.
"To Stingo with Love: An Author's Perspective on Writing Outside One's Culture." *New Advocate* 9 (Winter 1996): 1–7.
Letter to the Editor. *New Advocate* 9 (Summer 1996): vii–ix.
"Keyhole Fiction." SIGNAL 21 (Spring 1997): 5–10.

Secondary Works

Biographical and Critical Studies

About Kathryn Lasky. Publicity brochure. New York: Scholastic, 1997.
Donavin, Denise Perry. "The *Booklist* Interview." *Booklist* (October 1, 1991): 246–47.
"Kathryn Lasky." In Anne Commire, ed. *Something about the Author.* Vol. 14. Detroit: Gale Research, 1987, 124–25.
"Kathryn Lasky." In Donna Olendorf, ed. *Something about the Author.* Vol. 69. Detroit: Gale Research, 1992, 129–32.
"Kathryn Lasky." In Donald Gallo, ed. *Speaking for Ourselves.* Urbana, Ill.: NCTE, 1990, 114–15.
Samuels, Barbara. "Kathryn Lasky." In Ted Hipple, ed. *Writers for Young Adults.* Vol. 2. New York: Charles Scribner's Sons, 1997, 207–16.

Book Reviews: Young Adult Novels

THE NIGHT JOURNEY
Cooper, Ilene. *Booklist* (15 November 1981): 439
Hearne, Betsy. *Bulletin of the Center for Children's Books* (December 1981): 72
Heins, Ethel L. *Horn Book* (April 1982): 166.
Kennerley, Peter. *School Librarian* (June 1983): 144.

BEYOND THE DIVIDE
Babbitt, Natalie. *New York Times Book Review* (21 August 1983): 26.
Bulletin of the Center for Children's Books (June 1983): 192.
Lettus, Dorothy. *VOYA* (October 1983): 204.

THE BONE WARS
Frey, Yvonne A. *School Library Journal* (November 1988): 126.

Publishers Weekly (25 November 1988): 67.
Sutherland, Zena. *Bulletin of the Center for Children's Books* (November 1988): 77.
Terris, Susan. *New York Times Book Review* (18 December 1988): 30.

PRANK
Harrington, Pat. *School Library Journal* (October 1984): 168.
Mitchell, Judith. *VOYA* (February 1985): 328.
Schwartz, Albert V. *Interracial Books for Children Bulletin* (1 November 1985): 7.

HOME FREE
Bulletin of the Center for Children's Books (February 1986): 112.
Cooper, Ilene. *Booklist* (15 January 1986): 758.
Duncan, Marijo. *VOYA* (October 1986): 176.
Miller, Sara. *School Library Journal* (March 1986): 145.

PAGEANT
Endicott, Alba Quinones. *English Journal* (April 1992): 42.
Rochman, Hazel. *Beyond Borders* (Chicago: American Library Association, 1993), 201.
Wilms, Denise M. *Booklist* (15 November 1986): 507.

MEMOIRS OF A BOOKBAT
Blasi, Mary Jane. *The New Advocate* (Fall 1994): 296.
Crawford, Kathleen et al. *The Reading Teacher* (April 1995): 600.
Farmer, Lesley. *The Book Report* (November 1994): 45.
Kirkus Reviews (1 June 1994): 776.
Publishers Weekly (23 May 1994): 90.
Rochman, Hazel. *Booklist* (15 April 1994): 1526.
Smith, Alice Casey. *School Library Journal* (July 1994): 119.

BEYOND THE BURNING TIME
Burns, Mary M. *Horn Book* (March 1995): 200.
Kirkus Reviews (15 October 1994): 1410.
Noah, Carolyn. *School Library Journal* (January 1995): 108.
Publishers Weekly (17 October 1994): 82.

TRUE NORTH
Kirkus Reviews (1 October 1996): 1470.
Schene, Carol. *School Library Journal* (December 1996): 139.
Simonetti, Karen. *Booklist* (15 November 1996): 579.

Book Reviews: Fiction for Younger Readers

SHADOWS IN THE WATER
Publishers Weekly (2 November 1992): 72.

A VOICE IN THE WIND
Halverstadt, Julie. *School Library Journal* (December 1993): 114.

A Journey to the New World: The Diary of Remember Patience Whipple
Hawkins, Lynne B. *VOYA* (October 1996): 210.
Pine, Susan. *School Library Journal* (August 1996): 144.

Book Reviews: Nonfiction for Younger Readers

Sugaring Time
Cullinane, Jane F. *School Library Journal* (May 1983): 3.

Traces of Life
Camper, Cathryn A. *School Library Journal* (June 1990): 132.
Hearne, Betsy. *Bulletin of the Center for Children's Books* (June 1990): 245.
Luoma, *New York Times Book Review* (24 June 1990): 29.
Mandel, Ellen. *Booklist* (1 May 1990): 1707.

Dinosaur Dig
Browne, Malcolm W. *New York Times Book Review* (24 June 1990): 28.
Camper, Cathryn A. *School Library Journal* (May 1990): 98.

Surtsey: The Newest Place on Earth
Sutton, Roger. *Bulletin of the Center for Children's Books* (February 1993): 181.
Zvirin, Stephanie. *Booklist* (1 June 1993): 805.

Think Like an Eagle
Fader, Ellen. *School Library Journal* (April 1992): 138.
Hearne, Betsy. *Bulletin of the Center for Children's Books* (March 1992): 73.

Monarchs
Bush, Margaret A. *Horn Book* (November/December 1993): 755.
Oliver, Susan. *School Library Journal* (September 1993): 244.

Days of the Dead
Meudell, Jessie. *School Library Journal* (October 1994): 135.
Sutton, Roger. *Bulletin of the Center for Children's Books* (October 1994): 54.

The Most Beautiful Roof in the World: Exploring the Rainforest Canopy
Donavin, Denise Perry. *Booklist* (15 May 1986): 1360.

She's Wearing a Dead Bird on Her Head
Schott, Joanne. *Quill Quire* (November 1995): 47.

The Librarian Who Measured the Earth
Engelfried. *School Library Journal* (September 1994): 209.
Schott, Joanne. *Quill Quire* (November 1995): 47.

Book Reviews: Adult Fiction and Nonfiction

ATLANTIC CIRCLE
Buckley, Christopher. *New York Times Book Review* (10 February 1985): 15.
Ebershoff-Coles, Susan. *Library Journal* (December 1984): 2278.

TRACE ELEMENTS
Donavin, Denise Perry. *Booklist* (15 May 1986): 1360.
Maio, Kathleen. *Wilson Library Bulletin* 61 (December 1986): 53.
Publishers Weekly (18 April 1986): 51.

WIDOW OF OZ
Donavin, Denise Perry. *Booklist* (1 June 1989): 1696.
Publishers Weekly (21 April 1989): 81.

DARK SWAN
Donavin, Denise Perry. *Booklist* (1 June 1994): 1777.
Spencer, Pam. *School Library Journal* (March 1995): 235.

Index

accuracy in historical fiction, 48–53
adolescence, 37–38; in fiction, 129–30; in historical fiction, 100–101
adventure/accomplishment romances, 100
Alice Rose and Sam (Kathryn Lasky), 43, 140–41; historical accuracy in, 50
American West. *See Beyond the Divide; Bone Wars, The; Alice Rose and Sam*
apart. *See* independence
assimilation, 65
Atlantic Circle (Kathryn Lasky), 15–16
Audubon Society. *See* Massachusetts Audubon Society
Austen, Jane, 78
authenticity. *See* cultural authenticity
autism, 112–13

Babbitt, Natalie, 81
Baby for Max, A (Kathryn Lasky and Christopher Knight), 27–28
"bargain in the sky," 12–13
Beatty, John, 51
Beatty, Patricia, 51
Beyond the Burning Time (Kathryn Lasky), 141–49; characterization in, 144–46; critical reception, 56–57, 148–49; historical accuracy in, 49; keyhole history approach in, 143–44; narration in, 146–47; plot, 141–46; religion in, 145; sexuality in, 147; structure of, 146; witchcraft trials in, 143–46, 147–48

Beyond the Divide (Kathryn Lasky), 28, 69–80; characterization in, 70–73; compared to *The Night Journey,* 70–71, 77, 80–81; critical reception, 56, 81–82; freedom in, 79; historical accuracy in, 49; journeys in, 71–72, 73–74; language in, 77, 78–79; narrative shift in, 81; plot, 70–73; portrayal of Native Americans in, 74–78; rape in, 78–79; setting, 70, 80; survival in, 79–80; women in, 78–79
bigotry, 104–5
biographies, 43–46; cultural authenticity in, 45–46
Black Elk, 83, 84
Blos, Joan, 51–52
Bone Wars, The (Kathryn Lasky), 28–29, 82–93; critical reception, 90–91; dialect in, 92; evolutionary science in, 86; historical accuracy in, 49–50; independence in, 86; journeys in, 84; land ownership in, 89; language in, 90; Manifest Destiny in, 89; narrative shift in, 92; Native Americans in, 84–87, 88–89; paleontology in, 82, 89; plot, 82–83; prostitution in, 91–92; visions in, 84–85
Booklist: on *Dark Swan,* 36; on *Home Free,* 118; on *Memoirs of a Bookbat,* 138; on *The Most Beautiful Roof in the World,* 34; on *The Night Journey,* 61; on *Pageant,* 127;

Booklist (continued)
  on *Trace Elements*, 36; on *Traces of Life*, 30; on *True North*, 99; on *The Widow of Oz*, 129
Book Report: on *Memoirs of a Bookbat*, 138
Brilliant Streak, A (Kathryn Lasky), 44–45
Bruff, J. Goldsborough, 81
Buckley, Christopher, 16
Bulletin of the Center for Children's Books: on *Beyond the Divide*, 81–82; on *The Bone Wars*, 91; on *Home Free*, 118; on *Memoirs of a Bookbat*, 139; on *The Night Journey*, 61; on *Surtsey*, 33; on *Traces of Life*, 30
Bush, Margaret A., 33–34

Camper, Cathryn, 30
Campion Towers (John Beatty and Patricia Beatty), 51
Canby, Henry Seidel, 55
Catrow, David, 32
censorship, 134; and cultural authenticity, 45; in *Memoirs of a Bookbat*, 140
characterization: in adult mysteries, 37–39; in *Beyond the Burning Time*, 144–46; in *Beyond the Divide*, 70–73; in Calista Jacobs mysteries, 36; in *Home Free*, 113–14; in *Memoirs of a Bookbat*, 137–38; in *The Night Journey*, 61–2; in *Pageant*, 124–26; in *Prank*, 103–4, 106–7; in Starbuck twins books, 39, 40, 41; in *True North*, 96–97
Charpentier, Meredith, 27, 46; on *Pageant*, 127; on title of *The Night Journey*, 58
Chesterton, G. K., 38
Children's Book Guild Nonfiction Award, 27
cinema verité, 14
Clemens, Samuel, 43, 44–45, 50, 140–41
Cloud Eyes (Kathryn Lasky), 32
contemporary fiction, families in, 102. *See also* fiction; historical fiction

Cooper, Ilene, 61
Cullinane, Jane F., 27
cultural authenticity, 45
Custer, General George Armstrong, 83

Dark Swan (Kathryn Lasky), 36
Days of the Dead (Kathryn Lasky and Christopher Knight), 34
Dear America series, 42–43, 51. *See also Dreams in the Golden Country; Journey to the New World, A*
dialect, 92, 96
diaries, 52–54
Dinosaur Dig (Kathryn Lasky and Christopher Knight), 30–31
discontinuity, 105
Dollmaker (Kathryn Lasky and Christopher Knight), 25
Donavin, Denise Perry, 20, 36, 129
Donelson, Kenneth, 81, 100
Donne, John, 106
Double Trouble Squared (Kathryn Lasky), 39, 41–42
Dreams in the Golden Country (Kathryn Lasky), 42–43; diary format in, 52–53

eagles, 111–12, 114, 117
Ebershoff-Coles, Susan, 16
empowerment, 124–26
Endicott, Alba Quinones, 127
environmentalism, 18, 43–44, 112–13
equality, 43–44
Eratosthenes, 44
evolutionary science, 86

Fader, Ellen, 33
families, 4; in contemporary fiction, 102; in *Memoirs of a Bookbat*, 136–37; as nonfiction theme, 61–62; in *Pageant*, 122, 124; in *Prank*, 102–3, 107
fantasy, 116–18
Farmer, Lesley, 138
fiction: children's fiction, 17–19, 31–32; diary format, 52–54; themes, 18, 29–32, 37–38; young adult, 31.

See also contemporary fiction; historical fiction
Fourth of July Bear (Kathryn Lasky), 18
freedom, 79
Frey, Yvonne A., 90
friendship: in *Home Free,* 111, 112–14; in *Memoirs of a Bookbat,* 137
Frost, Robert, 81
fundamentalism, religious: in fiction, 149; in *Memoirs of a Bookbat,* 132–36, 139–40; in *Mortal Words,* 134

Gates, Henry Louis, 45
Gates of the Wind, The (Kathryn Lasky), 32
Gathering of Days, A (Joan Blos), 51–52
gender, 97–98
"guerilla": in *Beyond the Burning Time,* 144; in *Memoirs of a Bookbat,* 132; in *Pageant,* 125

Hall, Minna, 43
Harris, Violet J., 45–46
Harvard Divinity School, 10
Hawkins, Lynne B., 54
Hearne, Betsy, 30
Hemenway, Harriet, 43
Hercules (Kathryn Lasky), 32
historical fiction, 42–43, 47–67, 99–101; accuracy in, 48–53; adventure/accomplishment romances, 100; American West in, 68–82; critical reception, 56–57; first person narration in, 51–54; interpretive nature of, 55; keyhole approach, 47–48, 56, 142–43; themes in, 54–58, 60–65, 68, 100–101. *See also* contemporary fiction; fiction
Hoess, Rudolph, 104
Holocaust, 103–6
home, 114–15
Home Free (Kathryn Lasky), 18, 33, 111–19; autism in, 112–13; characterization in, 113–14; critical reception, 118–19; eagles in, 111–12, 114, 117; environmentalism in, 112–13; fantasy in, 116–18; friendship in, 111, 112–14; home in, 114–15; independence in, 113; language in, 115; narrative shifts in, 118; plot, 111–13; religion in, 116; setting, 116; structure of, 116
Horn Book: on *Beyond the Burning Time,* 149; on *Monarchs,* 33–34; on *The Night Journey,* 66–67
Horn Book Guide: on *Memoirs of a Bookbat,* 138

Idylls of the King (Alfred, Lord Tennyson), 123
I Have an Aunt on Marlborough Street (Kathryn Lasky), 32
I Have Four Names for My Grandfather (Kathryn Lasky and Christopher Knight), 14
immigration, 57
independence, 18; in *The Bone Wars,* 86; in *Home Free,* 113; in *The Night Journey,* 62; in *Pageant,* 121–22; in *Prank,* 107–8
Indians, portrayal of: in *Beyond the Divide,* 74–78; in *The Bone Wars,* 83, 84–87
Interracial Books for Children Bulletin, 110

Jefferson Cup Award, 43
Jem's Island (Kathryn Lasky), 18
Jewish experience: Holocaust, 103–6; in *The Night Journey,* 58, 60, 62–65; in *Pageant,* 119–21; persecution of, 58, 60, 62–65; in *Prank,* 103–6
Jolly, Allison, 35
journeys, 58–60; in *Beyond the Divide,* 71–72, 73–74; in *The Bone Wars,* 84–85; in historical fiction, 100; in *The Night Journey,* 58–60
Journey to the New World, A (Kathryn Lasky), 16, 42, 57; diary format in, 52–54

Kennerley, Peter, 61
"keyhole history," 47–48, 56, 142–43
Kirkus Reviews: on *Beyond the Burning Time,* 148–49; on *Memoirs of a Bookbat,* 139; on *True North,* 99

Knight, Christopher (husband of Kathryn Lasky), 10–12; collaboration with Kathryn Lasky, 1, 3, 14–15, 26–28, 32–35; as pilot, 12–13
Knight, Kathryn Lasky. *See* Lasky, Kathryn
Knight, Max (son of Kathryn Lasky), 16, 27–28, 131–32
Knight, Meribah (daughter of Kathryn Lasky), 1, 3, 16–17, 28

land ownership, 89
language: in *Beyond the Divide*, 77, 78–79; in *The Bone Wars*, 90; in *Home Free*, 115; in *Prank*, 106; in *True North*, 96
Lasky, Hortense (mother of Kathryn Lasky), 4–5
Lasky, Kathryn, 1, 3, 15; "Atlantic Circle" years, 13–16; on *The Bone Wars*, 90, 92; on book reviews, 46; books in progress, 43; on censorship, 134; childhood, 3–7; children's fiction, 17–19, 31–32; collaboration with Christopher Knight, 14–15, 26–28, 32–35; on cultural authenticity, 45–46; early non-fiction works, 19–21; early years of marriage, 11–16; fact and fiction in work, 29–31; at Harvard Divinity School, 10; on historical fiction, 47–48, 55–56; on historical research, 28–29; home in Cambridge, 23–25; "landscape gene," 66, 68; on "packaging" mentality in publishing, 40; on *Pageant*, 119–20, 126; parenthood and, 16–17; on religion, 126, 131; response to criticism, 56–57; on school, 5–7; at *Town and Country*, 7–10; on Twain, Mark, 50; on *The Widow of Oz*, 129; as writer in many genres, 19–20
Lasky, Marven (father of Kathryn Lasky), 3–4, 5
Leit, Anne, 46
Leucothea, 12, 13, 15, 17
Librarian Who Measured the Earth, The (Kathryn Lasky), 44

Library Journal: on *Atlantic Circle*, 16
Literature for Today's Young Adults (Alleen Pace Nilsen and Kenneth Donelson), 81, 100
Lowman, Meg, 34
Luoma, Jon R., 30

Mallon, Thomas, 48
Mandel, Ellen, 30
Manifest Destiny, 89
mapmaking, 73–74
Marven of the Great North Woods (Kathryn Lasky), 3–4
Massachusetts Audubon Society, 43
Memoirs of a Bookbat (Kathryn Lasky), 131–40; censorship in, 140; characterization in, 137–38; critical reception, 138–40; families in, 136–37; friendship in, 137; plot, 132–37; religion in, 132–136, 139–40
mimetic fiction, 127
Mist over Athelney (Geoffrey Trease), 48–49
Monarchs (Kathryn Lasky and Christopher Knight), 33–34
Moore, Marianne, 48
Morrison, Samuel Eliot, 19
Mortal Words (Kathryn Lasky), 36
Most Beautiful Roof in the World, The (Kathryn Lasky and Christopher Knight), 34–35
multiculturalism, 45–46
Mumbo Jumbo (Kathryn Lasky), 36
My Island Grandmother (Kathryn Lasky), 17–18
My Name is America series, 43
mysteries: Calista Jacobs books, 35–39, 134; Starbuck twins books, 36, 39–42
myths, heroic, 68

narration: in *Beyond the Burning Time*, 146–47; in historical fiction, 51–54; in *The Night Journey*, 66; in *Pageant*, 127; in *Prank*, 105; in *True North*, 94

Index

narrative point of view: in *Beyond the Burning Time*, 147; in *Beyond the Divide*, 81; in *The Bone Wars*, 92; in *Home Free*, 118
Native Americans: in *Beyond the Divide*, 74–78, in *The Bone Wars*, 83, 84–87
New Advocate: on cultural authenticity, 45; on *Memoirs of a Bookbat*, 138–39
New Yorker, 7
New York Times: on *Atlantic Circle*, 16
New York Times Book Review: on *Beyond the Divide*, 81; on *The Bone Wars*, 90; on *Dinosaur Dig*, 30–31; on *Traces of Life*, 30
Night (Elie Wiesel), 104
Night Journey, The (Kathryn Lasky), 20, 58–67; characterization in, 61–65; compared to *Beyond the Divide*, 70–71, 77, 80–81; critical reception, 61, 66–67; narrative shift in, 66; selection of title, 58; setting, 66; structure, 65; themes, 58, 60, 61–65
Nilsen, Alleen Pace, 81, 100
Noah, Carolyn, 148
nonfiction, 19–21, 25–27; critical reception, 26–27; themes, 32–35

Oliver, Susan, 34
oppression: in *The Bone Wars*, 88–89; in *The Night Journey*, 62–65; in *Prank*, 103–6; in *True North*, 96

Pageant (Kathryn Lasky), 7, 119–28; as autobiographical work, 119–20; characterization in, 124–26; critical reception, 127–28; empowerment in, 124–26; families in, 122, 124; independence, 121–22; Jewish religion in, 119–21; narration of, 127; plot, 119, 122–24; politics in, 121; prejudice in, 120; racism in, 123; sexuality in, 121–24; structure, 121
paleontology, 29–31; in *The Bone Wars*, 82, 89
personal appearance, 102–3, 108
Pine, Susan, 53–54

plot: of *Beyond the Burning Time*, 141–46; *Beyond the Divide*, 70–73; in *The Bone Wars*, 82–83; of *Home Free*, 111–13; of *Memoirs of a Bookbat*, 132–37; of *Pageant*, 122–24; of *True North*, 94–95
politics, 121
Pond Year (Kathryn Lasky), 3, 32
popular culture, 108–9
"portrait biographies," 44
Prank (Kathryn Lasky), 12, 102–11; bigotry in, 104–5; characterization in, 103–4, 106–7; critical reception, 110; discontinuity, 105; families in, 102–3, 107; Holocaust in, 103–6; independence in, 107–8; language in, 106; narration in, 105; personal appearance in, 103–4, 108; plot, 102–4; popular culture in, 108–9; religion in, 109–10; self in, 108; sexuality in, 108
Pratt Library's Young Adult Advisory Board, 90
prejudice, 120
Pride and Prejudice (Jane Austen), 78
prostitution, 91–92
Publisher's Weekly: on *Beyond the Burning Time*, 149; on *The Bone Wars*, 90; on *Dark Swan*, 36; on *Memoirs of a Bookbat*, 138; on Starbuck twins books, 39; on *True North*, 99; on *The Widow of Oz*, 129
publishing industry, 40
Puppeteer (Kathryn Lasky and Christopher Knight), 25–26

Quill Quire: on *She's Wearing a Dead Bird on Her Head*, 44

racism, 123
rape, 78–79
Reading Teacher: on *Memoirs of a Bookbat*, 138
Reed, Arthea, 49
religion, 131; in *Beyond the Burning Time*, 145; in fiction, 149; in *Home Free*, 116; in *Memoirs of a Bookbat*, 132–36, 139–40; in *The Night Jour-*

ney, 64–65; in *Pageant*, 119–21; in *Prank*, 109–10
research, historical, 46
Rice, Anne, 132
Rochman, Hazel, 127, 149

satire, 36–37
Schlee, Ann, 54–55
Scholastic, 43
School Librarian: on *The Night Journey*, 61
School Library Journal: on *The Bone Wars*, 90; on *Dark Swan*, 36; on *Dinosaur Dig*, 30; on *Home Free*, 118; on *A Journey to the New World*, 53–54; on *The Librarian Who Measured the Earth*, 44; on *Monarchs*, 34; on *Sugaring Time*, 27; on *Think Like an Eagle*, 33; on *Traces of Life*, 30; on *True North*, 99; on *A Voice in the Wind*, 39
Schott, Joanne, 44
Schwartz, Albert, 110
Searching for Laura Ingalls (Kathryn Lasky and Christopher Knight), 1
Sea Swan (Kathryn Lasky), 18
"seizures of power," 54–55
self, 108
setting: of *Beyond the Divide*, 70, 80; of historical fiction, 99; of *Home Free*, 116; of *The Night Journey*, 66; of Starbuck twins books, 40–41
sexuality: in *Beyond the Burning Time*, 147; in *Pageant*, 121–24; in *Prank*, 108
Shadows in the Dawn (Kathryn Lasky and Christopher Knight), 35
Shadows in the Water (Kathryn Lasky), 40, 42
She's Wearing a Dead Bird on Her Head (Kathryn Lasky), 32, 43–44
Sioux Indians, 83, 84–85
slavery, 93–95, 98–99
social mores, 97
Solo (Kathryn Lasky), 32
spiritual exploration, 100
Starbuck twins books, 39–42
stereotypes, historical, 68

structure: of *Beyond the Burning Time*, 146; of *Home Free*, 116; of *The Night Journey*, 66; of *Pageant*, 121; of Starbuck twins books, 40; of *True North*, 94–95, 96
Sugaring Time (Kathryn Lasky and Christopher Knight), 25–26
Surtsey (Kathryn Lasky and Christopher Knight), 32–33
survival, 64; in *Beyond the Divide*, 79–80
Sutherland, Zena, 91
Sutton, Roger, 33
Swedberg, Jack, 33

Tall Ships (Kathryn Lasky), 19
Tantrum, The (Kathryn Lasky), 32
telepathy, 39
Terris, Susan, 90, 91
themes: children's mysteries, 41–42; fiction, 18, 29–33, 37–38; historical fiction, 54–58, 60–65, 68, 100–101; nonfiction, 32–35
Think Like an Eagle (Kathryn Lasky and Christopher Knight), 33
time, 99
time travel, 117–18
Town and Country, 7–10
Trace Elements (Kathryn Lasky), 36
Traces of Life (Kathryn Lasky and Christopher Knight), 29–30
Trease, Geoffrey, 48–49
True North (Kathryn Lasky), 93–99; characterization in, 96–97; critical reception, 99; gender in, 97–98; language in, 96; narration in, 94; oppression in, 96; plot, 94–95; slavery in, 93–95, 98–99; social mores in, 97; structure, 94–95, 96
Tudor Hall, 6–7
Tugboats Never Sleep (Kathryn Lasky and Christopher Knight), 14
Twain, Mark, 43, 44–45, 50, 140–41

Underground Railroad, 93–95

visions, 84–85

Index

Voice in the Wind, A (Kathryn Lasky), 39, 42
Voice of Youth Advocates: on *Beyond the Divide*, 82; on *Home Free*, 119

Walker, Sarah Breedlove, 45
Walsh, Jill Paton, 55
Washington Post, 27
Weaver's Gift, The (Kathryn Lasky and Christopher Knight), 25–26
Widow of Oz, The (Kathryn Lasky), 19, 128–29
Wiesel, Elie, 104

Wilder, Laura Ingalls. See *Searching for Laura Ingalls*
Wilms, Denise M., 127–28
witchcraft trials, 143–46, 147–48
women: in *Beyond the Divide*, 78–79; equal rights for, 43–44

Yana Indians, 73, 75–76
Young Adult Advisory Board (Pratt Library), 90
"Youth-to-Youth Books" (Young Adult Advisory Board, Pratt Library), 90

zealots. *See* fundamentalism

The Author

Joanne Brown is an associate professor of English at Drake University, where she teaches courses in adolescent literature, American drama, short fiction, and professional communication. Her articles on young adult fiction have appeared in the *Alan Review* and SIGNAL. She holds an undergraduate degree in theater and graduate degrees in English. She has also taught acting courses for children and adults.

The Editor

Patricia J. Campbell is an author and critic specializing in books for young adults. She has taught adolescent literature at UCLA and is the former assistant coordinator of Young Adult Services for the Los Angeles Public Library. Her literary criticism has been published in the *New York Times Book Review* and many other journals. From 1978 to 1988 her column "The YA Perplex," a monthly review of young adult books, appeared in the *Wilson Library Bulletin*. She now writes a column on controversial issues in adolescent literature, "The Sand in the Oyster," for *Horn Book* magazine. Recently she has been traveling the country to lead "YA Biblioramas," her intensive workshops on young adult fiction for teachers and librarians.

Campbell is the author of five books, among them *Presenting Robert Cormier*, the first volume in the Twayne Young Adult Authors Series. In 1989 she was the recipient of the American Library Association Grolier Award for distinguished achievement with young people and books. A native of Los Angeles, Campbell now lives on an avocado ranch near San Diego, where she and her husband, David Shore, write and publish books on overseas motor-home travel.